Money

Money

Ideology, History, Politics

Geoffrey Ingham

polity

First published in 2020 by Polity Press

Polity Press
65 Bridge Street
Cambridge CB2 1UR, UK

Polity Press
101 Station Landing
Suite 300
Medford, MA 02155, USA

ISBN-13: 978-1-5095-2681-9
ISBN-13: 978-1-5095-2682-6 (pb)

A catalogue record for this book is available from the British Library.

Library of Congress Cataloging-in-Publication Data

Names: Ingham, Geoffrey K., author.
Title: Money / Geoffrey Ingham.
Description: Medford : Polity, [2019] | Series: What is political economy? | Includes bibliographical references and index. | Summary: "Few economic phenomena provoke as much confusion as money. In this accessible book, Geoffrey Ingham cuts through this tangled web of debate to examine the fundamental debate over the nature of money and trace the import of these competing views for how we understand our contemporary monetary systems"-- Provided by publisher.
Identifiers: LCCN 2019023996 (print) | LCCN 2019023997 (ebook) | ISBN 9781509526819 (hardback) | ISBN 9781509526826 (paperback) | ISBN 9781509526857 (epub)
Subjects: LCSH: Money.
Classification: LCC HG221 .I524 2019 (print) | LCC HG221 (ebook) | DDC 332.4--dc23
LC record available at https://lccn.loc.gov/2019023996
LC ebook record available at https://lccn.loc.gov/2019023997

Typeset in 10.5 on 12pt Sabon by
Servis Filmsetting Ltd, Stockport, Cheshire
Printed and bound in Great Britain by CPI Group (UK) Ltd, Croydon

For further information on Polity, visit our website: politybooks.com

Contents

PART I

WHAT IS MONEY?

1
Money's Puzzles

The modern world without money is unimaginable. Most probably originating with literacy and numeracy, it is one of our most vital 'social technologies' (Ingham, 2004). Obviously, money is essential for the vast number of increasingly global economic transactions that take place; but it is much more than the economists' medium of exchange. Money is the link between the present and possible futures. A confident expectation that next week's money will be the same as today's allows us to map and secure society's myriad social, economic, and political linkages, including our individual positions, plotted by income, taxes, debts, insurance, pensions, and so on. Without money to record, facilitate, and plan, it would be impossible to create and maintain large-scale societies. In Felix Martin's apt analogy, money is the modern world's 'operating system' (Martin, 2013).

However, despite money's pivotal role in modern life, it is notoriously puzzling and the subject of unresolved – often rancorous – intellectual and political disputes that can be traced at least as far back as Aristotle and Plato in Classical Greece and the third century BCE in China (von Glahn, 1996). Many of the innumerable tracts and treatises on money begin with lists of quotations to illustrate people's bewilderment (see the fine selection in Kevin Jackson's *The Oxford Book of Money* [Jackson, 1995]). With characteristic whimsy, the great economist John Maynard Keynes (who knew a great deal about money) said that he was aware of only three people who understood it: one of his students; a professor at a foreign university; and a junior clerk at the Bank of England. The banker Baron Rothschild had made a similar observation a century earlier (quoted in Ingham, 2005, xi), adding that all three disagreed!

We shall see that one of the most puzzling and counterintuitive conceptions of money lies at the core of mainstream economics. We experience money as a powerful force; it 'makes the world go around' – and sometimes almost 'stop'. Governments stand in awe of monetary instability, constantly monitoring rates of inflation and foreign exchange, and levels of state and personal debt. Central banks strive to assure us that they can deliver 'sound money' and stability; but – like their predecessors – they are constantly thwarted. Paradoxically, however, from the standpoint of mainstream economic *theory*, money is not very important. In mathematical models of the economy, money is a 'neutral', or passive, element – a 'constant' not a 'variable'. Money is not an active force; it does no more than facilitate the process of production and exchange. Here, the sources of economic value are the 'real' factors of production: raw material, energy, labour, and especially technology; money does no more than measure these values and enable their exchange. This conception, which can be traced to Aristotle, had become the established orthodoxy by the eighteenth century. David Hume could confidently declare in his tract 'Of Money' (1752) that 'it is none of the wheels of trade. It is the oil which renders the motion of the wheels more smooth and easy' (quoted in Jackson, 1995, 3). A little later, in *The Wealth of Nations* (1776), Adam Smith consolidated the place of 'neutral money' in what became known as 'classical economics'.

Joseph Schumpeter's mid-twentieth-century identification of the differences between 'real' and 'monetary' analysis and his summary of the latter's assumptions has never been bettered:

> Real analysis proceeds from the principle that all essential phenomena of economic life are capable of being described in terms of goods and services, of decisions about them, and of relations between them. Money enters into the picture only in the modest role of a

technical device . . . in order to facilitate transactions. . . . [S]o long as it functions normally, it does not affect the economic process, which behaves in the same way as it would in a barter economy: this is essentially what the concept of Neutral Money implies. Thus, money has been called a 'garb' or 'veil' over the things that really matter. . . . Not only *can* it be discarded whenever we are analyzing the fundamental features of the economic process but it *must* be discarded just as a veil must be drawn aside if we are to see the face behind it. Accordingly, money prices must give way to the ratios between the commodities that are the really important thing 'behind' money prices. (Schumpeter 1994 [1954], 277, original emphasis)

This view remains at the core of modern mainstream macro-economics, which argues that money does not influence 'real' factors in the long run: that is, productive forces – especially advances in *material* technology – are ultimately the source of economic value. Therefore, '[f]or many purposes . . . monetary neutrality is approximately correct' (Mankiw and Taylor, 2008, 126, which is a representative text). However, there is an alternative view: 'monetary analysis' follows a view of money which prevailed in the practical world of business before the classical economists' theoretical intervention (Hodgson, 2015). Here money is money-*capital* – a dynamic independent economic force. Money is not merely Hume's 'oil' for economic 'wheels'; it is, rather, the '*social* technology' without which the 'classical' economists' *physical* capital cannot be set in motion and developed. This distinction, between 'real' analysis and 'monetary' analysis, is known as the 'Classical Dichotomy'.

Money itself cannot create value; but in capitalism the wheels are not set in motion and production is not consumed without the necessary prior creation of money for investment, production, and consumption (see Smithin, 1918). In the 'classical' view, the 'real' economy is in fact an 'unreal' model of a pure *exchange*, or *market*, economy in which money is the medium for the exchange of commodities: that is, Commodity–Money–Commodity (C–M–C). Here, money enables individuals to gain *utility*: that is, satisfaction from the commodity. In 'real-world' capitalism, money is the goal of production – the realization of *money-profit* from the employment of money-capital and wage-labour: that is,

Money (capital)–Commodity–Money (profit) (M–C–M). As Marx and Keynes stressed, depressions and unemployment are not caused by the failure of 'real' productive forces. These can lie idle for want of money for investment and consumption not only in the immediate short term but also in the long run. And as Keynes scathingly remarked, the *'long run* is a misleading guide to current affairs. *In the long run* we are all dead. Economists set themselves too easy, too useless a task if in tempestuous seasons they can only tell us that when the storm is long past the ocean is flat again' (Keynes, 1971 [1923], 65, original emphasis).

For economic orthodoxy, the proponents of monetary analysis were 'cranks' who were banished to an academic and intellectual 'underground' (Keynes, 1973 [1936], 3, 32, 355; Goodhart, 2009). But, for Keynes, they were 'brave heretics' whose analysis was revived and greatly elaborated in his *The General Theory of Employment, Interest and Money* (1936). A late nineteenth-century American 'crank', Alexander Del Mar – unknown to Keynes – has only recently come to light (Zarlenga, 2002). He anticipated Keynes's general position on monetary theory and policy:

> Money is a Measure ... the Unit of money is All Money within a given legal jurisdiction. ... The wheels of Industry are at this moment clogged, and what clogs them is that materialistic conception which mistakes a piece of metal for the measure of an ideal relation, a measure that resides not at all in the metal, but in the numerical relation of the piece to the set of pieces to which it is legally related, whether of metal, or paper, or both combined. (Del Mar, 1901, 8)

Keynes sought theoretically to convince his 'classical' orthodox mentors and colleagues that government expenditure, financed by money created in advance of tax revenue, could solve chronic unemployment in the 1930s. Money created by government spending would increase production and employment, which, in turn, would increase 'effective aggregate demand': that is, real 'purchasing power'. As opposed to the subjective 'wants' and 'preferences' of orthodox economic theory, demand created by expenditure was both 'effective' and 'aggregate', inaugurating a positive cycle of growth and tax revenue to fund the original deficit. For a while during and after the Second World War, Keynesian versions of 'monetary analysis' gained acceptance in theory and policy. However, as we shall see, the 1970s crises were held to have discredited Keynesian economics, leading to a revival of the old orthodoxy of 'neutral' money and the 'real' economy.

The two kinds of economic analysis and their respective theories of money lie behind arguably this most contested question in the governance of capitalism. On the one hand, mainstream economics believes that the supply of money may have a *short-run* positive effect, but cannot and therefore should not exceed the economy's productive capacity in the *long run*. Only 'real' forces of production – technology, labour – create new value, and their input cannot be increased simply by injections of money. Consequently, if monetary expansion runs ahead of these 'real' forces, inflation inevitably follows. On the other hand, the broadly Keynesian and heterodox tradition continues to argue that money is the vital productive resource – a 'social technology' – that can be used to create non-inflationary economic growth and employment.

However, it is of the utmost importance that the theoretical dispute is not seen exclusively as an 'academic' question; theories of money are also ideological. Our understanding of money's nature – what it is and how it is produced – is intimately bound up with conflict over who should control its creation and, by implication, how it is used. Insisting that money is nothing more than a 'neutral' element in the economy implies that it can be safely removed from politics. If money were merely a passive instrument for measuring pre-existing values of commodities and enabling their exchange, then disputes over its use would be misguided. All we need to do is ensure that there is enough money for it to fulfil its functions and ensure the smooth operation of the economic system – which is precisely how the money question is most frequently posed. The retired Governor of the Bank of England, Mervyn King, wrote in his recent memoirs that "[in essence] . . . the role of a central bank is extremely simple: to ensure that the right amount of money is created in both good and bad times" (King, 2017, xxi). The quantity of money should be calibrated to enable the consumption of what has been produced. Too little money will depress activity as goods cannot be bought; and too much money will do no more than inflate prices.

Here we encounter another of money's many puzzles. From a *theoretical* standpoint, it might be a simple matter to supply the right amount of money, but *in practice* it is not. We shall see that the experiment with 'monetarist' policy to control the money supply in the 1980s was beset by two related problems (see chapter 4). Confronted by the complexity of different forms of money in modern capitalism, the monetary authorities were unsure about what should count as money and how it should be counted. Notes and coins – cash – were an insignificant component of the money supply. But which of the other forms of money – bank accounts, deposits – and forms of credit – credit cards and private IOUs used in financial networks – should be included? Furthermore, many of the non-cash forms were beyond the control of the monetary authorities (see chapter 6).

Despite monetary authorities' many obvious practical and technical problems in conducting 'monetary policy' – essentially, attempting to control inflation – the *long-run neutrality* of money remains a core assumption of most mainstream economics. To believe otherwise – that money can be used as an independent creative force – is to suffer from the 'money illusion'. As we shall see, the 'illusion' is to think that money has powers beyond its function as a simple instrument that only measures existing value and enables economic exchange. However, the centuries-old persistence and intensity of the unresolved disputes tells us that money is not merely this technical device to be managed by economic experts. Rather, it is also a source of social power to get things done ('infrastructural power') and to control people ('despotic power') (Ingham, 2004, 4). The 'money question' lies at the centre of all political struggles about the kind of society we want and how it might be achieved.

In the late nineteenth and early twentieth centuries, the longstanding intellectual, ideological, and political debates on money became embroiled in an acrimonious academic dispute about the most appropriate methods for the study of society, which ultimately led to the formation of the distinct disciplines of economics and sociology (Ingham, 2004). In 1878, exasperated by the endless wrangling, American economist Francis Amasa Walker decided on a deceptively simple solution (see Schumpeter, 1994 [1954], 1086): 'money is what money does', which he described in terms of four functions:

1 *money of account/measure of value*: a numerical measure of value and for economic calculation; pricing offers of goods and debt contracts; recording income and wealth;
2 a *means of payment*: for settling all debts that are denominated in the same money of account;
3 a *medium of exchange*: something that can be exchanged for all other commodities;
4 a *store of value*: a repository of purchasing and debt settling power, enabling deferment of consumption and investment or simply saving 'for a rainy day'.

This list is still found almost without exception in today's textbooks. Its longevity gives the impression that the money question has been settled, but this is far from the case. Although it is obvious that money does these things, matters are not quite as simple as Walker had hoped. His solution masked the difficulties and confusions that had caused his and many others' exasperation. Schumpeter correctly saw that the main reason for the unresolved disagreements was that the *commodity* and *claim (credit)* theories of money, including their respective 'real' and 'monetary' analyses, were by their very nature 'incompatible' (Schumpeter, 1917, 649). We should add that he also saw that the two theories were often inconsistent and contradictory, obscuring their differences and making 'views on money as difficult to describe as shifting clouds' (Schumpeter, 1994 [1954], 289). These theories are examined in the following chapter; here we need only note the basic differences.

In the simplest terms, the main points of contention reflect two longstanding general intellectual positions: *materialism* and *naturalism* versus *nominalism* and *social constructionism*. On the one hand, did money, as a *medium of exchange*, originate in barter as the intrinsically valuable *material commodity* that could be exchanged for all others? For example, during the debate on the reform of the monetary system in the late nineteenth century, the US Monetary Commission in

1877 concluded that value 'inheres in the quality of the material thing, and not in mental estimation' (quoted in Carruthers and Babb, 1996, 550). The Commission favoured following the British 'gold standard', in which currency comprised the issue of gold coins, such as the £1 sovereign, and the promise that all paper notes with a face value of £1 were 'convertible': that is, exchangeable in an officially declared weight of gold. (Present-day British paper currency carries the anachronistic pledge 'I promise to pay the bearer on demand the sum of [*x*] pounds': that is, the sum in gold at a rate declared by the Bank of England; see chapter 4.) By the end of the nineteenth century, an increasing number of countries adopted the gold standard, which linked their currency's exchange rates to the common standard and facilitated participation in the international trading system based in London.

On the other hand, a minority rejected the view of the US Commission and held that money was precisely a 'mental estimation': that is, a *socially and politically* constructed *abstract value* (Del Mar, 1901). Soon after, in a critique of the dominant materialist conception of commodity money at the zenith of the gold standard era, Alfred Mitchell Innes concurred, declaring that "[t]he eye has never seen, nor the hand touched a dollar. All that we can touch or see is a promise to pay or satisfy a debt due for an amount called a dollar [which is] intangible, immaterial, abstract" (Mitchell Innes, 1914, 358). The dollar debt was settled by a *token credit*: that is, a *means of payment* which constituted a *claim* on goods offered for sale in a dollar monetary system. *The existence of a debt gives money its value.* As Georg Simmel explained, around the same time, in his sociological classic *The Philosophy of Money*, '[M]oney is only a claim upon society . . . the owner of money possesses such a claim and by transferring it to whoever performs the service, he directs him to an anonymous producer who, on the basis of his membership of the community, offers the required service in exchange for the money' (Simmel, 1978 [1907], 177–8).

Furthermore, 'claim' (or 'credit') theory and 'commodity-exchange' offered diametrically opposed analyses of banking. 'Commodity-exchange' theorists saw bankers as intermediaries collecting small pools of money from savers and lending it from the accumulated reservoirs to borrowers. Nothing was added to the supply of money; banks enabled it to be used more efficiently (see Schumpeter, 1994 [1954], 1110–17). However, it was obvious that something more mysterious was at work in banking. How could savers and borrowers still have use of the same fixed and finite quantity of money? As we will see in chapters 3 and 4, claim (or credit) theory was more closely associated with the view that 'the banker is not so much primarily a middleman in the commodity "purchasing power" as a *producer* of this commodity' (Schumpeter, 1934, 74, emphasis added). We shall see in chapter 4 that capitalist banking originated in early modern Europe and other commercially developed regions from use of 'bills of exchange' and other acknowledgements of debt (IOUs) issued by merchants as means of payment within their trading networks. Gradually, these evolved into interdependent banking giros: that is, networks in which the banks borrowed from each other and extended loans to clients – especially to the emerging states. Unlike money-lending, where loans depleted the stock of coined money, the bankers' loans comprised newly *created* credit money based on trust and confidence in their business. A *deposit* would be created in the borrower's account by a stroke of the banker's pen from which the borrower could draw banknotes (IOUs) in payment to third parties. Their acceptance was based on the issuing bank's promise to accept them in payment of any debt owed. In their double-entry bookkeeping, the loan (deposit in the borrower's account) was the bank's *asset* (debt owed by the borrower) balanced by the borrower's *liability* (debt owed to the bank). Banks also borrowed from each other in the giro to balance their books. In this way, money could be produced by the *expansion of debt and the promise of repayment* as represented in double-entry bookkeeping, which, in turn, represents the *social relation of credit and debt*. In modern economics, this is referred to as 'endogenous' money creation as opposed to the 'exogenous' production of currency outside the market by governments and central banks.

Walker merely sidestepped the 'incompatibility' by smuggling the two antithetical conceptions of money into the list as different 'functions' of the *same* thing: money. After a century in textbooks, it is now widely assumed – if even given a second thought – that the differences between *medium of exchange* and *means of payment* and *money* and *credit* are semantic. Are they not different terms for the same thing? Surely, common sense dictates that handing over a coin for goods is simultaneously *exchange* and *payment*. This imagery of physical – minted or printed – money persists in the era of 'virtual' money transmitted through cyberspace. We shall see that digital money causes much common sense and academic confusion. Bitcoins, for example, are represented by the image of precisely what they are not: a material 'coin'. What will be the consequences if digital money replaces cash? If money is a medium of exchange, what is 'exchanged' when a card is 'swiped' across a terminal as a means of payment? Doesn't this rather involve the use of a token 'credit', carried or transmitted by the card – which is retained – to cancel a debt incurred briefly by the purchaser?

Finally, defining money by its functions raises further questions: does something have to perform *all* the functions to be money? In other words, is 'moneyness' constituted by all the functions? For example, there are better stores of value than money. If not all the functions are necessary to confer 'moneyness', do any take primacy? In commodity theory, money is essentially a *medium of exchange* on which all other functions depend. We shall see in the following chapter that two of the functions in Walker's list – *medium of exchange* and *means of payment* – are integral parts of two radically different theories of money. On the one hand, intrinsically valuable material commodities can become widely used *media of exchange* in bilateral trades: that is, bartered. On the other hand, *means of payment* refers to a token of credit that can settle a debt incurred by the purchase of something because the value of both credit and debt is denominated in the same *money of account*. The numismatist Philip Grierson illustrates the difference between *medium of exchange* and *means of payment*, which he takes to be 'money', with the example of fur trappers in eighteenth-century Virginia who carried twists of tobacco to be exchanged for food and lodging on their journeys. The ratio of tobacco and food and lodging varied considerably in different exchanges and the tobacco only became 'money' when its value was denominated in a *money of account*: that is, at 5 shillings an ounce (Grierson, 1977).

We shall see in the following chapter that the two theories – 'commodity-exchange' and 'credit theory' – contain irreconcilable explanations of how the denomination of nominal face value of money – *money of account/measure of value* – originates. In this regard, Keynes was intrigued by the fact that circa 4000 BCE, Babylon did not have a circulating currency of material 'things', but used a nominal *money of account* to measure the value of stocks of commodities and to denominate contracts and wages. The first known circulation of *material* forms of coined *commodity* money came some 3,000 years later in Lydia around 700 BCE. One of the questions to be explored in the following chapters is whether 'moneyness' – that is, the specific and distinctive quality of money – is conferred *nominally* by its designation in the money of account or *materially* by the precious metals' 'intrinsic' value or the pre-existing value of commodities in the 'real' economy. The era of precious metal money has gone; none the less, we shall see that the opposition between 'nominalist' and 'materialist' theories continues to lie behind academic disputes on the nature of money.

A preoccupation with narrow economic functions diverts attention from a range of important questions for which the two theories also provide further 'incompatible' answers. First, how can money perform its functions? Orthodox economics infers that the rational individual uses money for the self-evident advantages of the functions in Walker's list. However, these functions are only fulfilled if *everyone else* simultaneously sees the advantage, but this cannot be explained in terms of individual rationality. It may be rational to hold the things that fulfil the functions if they are *intrinsically valuable commodities* but not *token* credits. As we shall see, money's functions require a different explanation.

Second, money is not only a 'social technology'; it is also a source of power – 'infrastructural' and 'despotic' power. Obviously, the *accumulation* of money confers power; but the power to *create* money is of more fundamental importance. Money-creating power is an essential element of state sovereignty; yet we shall see that in modern capitalism this power is shared with the banking system. Here, the dual nature of money's power as an 'infrastructural' public resource and a means of 'despotic' domination becomes apparent. We have noted that modern money can be produced by the creation of debt, which necessarily entails an inequality of power between creditors and debtors (Graeber, 2011; Hager 2016). A central theme of the book will follow the lead given by the great sociologist Max Weber, who interpreted modern capitalism as 'the struggle for economic existence', in which money is a 'weapon' wielded by conflicting interests to achieve their aims and strengthen their position as much as it is a public good for pursuing our collective welfare (Weber, 1978, 93).

Today, we are encouraged to believe that the questions of who creates money and for what ends and in what quantities are technical matters to be decided by experts; but they are political questions. As we have noted, the control of money creation lies behind major political struggles in the representative democracies. Those in favour of monetary expansion to finance employment and consumption – the broad Keynesian camp – are opposed by those who place the avoidance of inflation as the main priority of monetary policy. Furthermore, there is no single definitive rational means of deciding between them. Whichever route is taken depends on which school of economic theory and conception of money is chosen, which, in turn, is related to different interests in society: for example, debtors versus creditors; possessors of accumulated money wealth (rentiers) versus those dependent on the employment of their intellectual and physical labour – 'Wall Street' versus 'Main Street', as the question was posed during the Great Financial Crisis in 2008. Most academic theories of money – especially those held in most orthodox and mainstream schools of economics – fail entirely to address the question of money and power: that is, to register that money is a question of *political economy*.

The following chapter explores these astonishingly persistent intellectual disputes and their impact on the conflict over who should create money and control how it is used. Chapter 3 draws the theoretical discussion together in a summary of a social theory of money which is used to frame a brief account of Weimar Germany's severe hyperinflationary crisis, where money's social and political foundations are 'unveiled' (Orléan, 2008). Chapter 4 continues the twin themes – theories of money and struggle for its control – in an account of the development from the sixteenth century onwards in western Europe of the distinctive system of shared money creation in capitalism created 'exogenously' by states and 'endogenously' by private banks.

Chapters 5 and 6 examine how this dual monetary sovereignty and capitalism's private contract law have resulted in complex and fragmented monetary systems comprising state-issued currency and bank credit money mediated by central banks; myriad 'near' moneys issued as IOUs by financial institutions; local community 'complementary' and 'alternative' currencies; and crypto-currencies such as Bitcoin. In chapter 7, we see that proposals for monetary reform raised by the Great Financial Crisis of 2008 remain informed by the unresolved intellectual disputes which mask and obfuscate the essentials of *the* money question: who should control its creation and how it is to be used. Some tentative observations are offered in the concluding chapter.

2
The 'Incompatibles': Commodity and Credit Theories

As we noted in the previous chapter, the earliest known coined form of money was minted in Lydia (now western Turkey) around 700 BCE. This was minted from a naturally occurring alloy of silver and gold (electrum) and spread quickly to Classical Greece. Here we find the first accounts of the dispute about the nature of money in the observations of Plato (428–348 BCE) and Aristotle (384–322 BCE). (See Peacock, 2013, for the most accessible, comprehensive account of early coinage and money.) In a critique of coined money's social and political impact, Aristotle contended that the pursuit of money as a means of power was unethical. Barter, which he believed had previously been the routine way of making transactions, was based on a mutually agreed exchange of commodities; but money could now be accumulated and used as a means for disruptive and corrupt political domination. Money, Aristotle argued, *should* be no more than a 'neutral' instrument: that is, a commodity used as a medium of exchange for transactions that increase the welfare of those involved. Plato's later criticism of the wasteful unnecessary use of precious metal as coins strongly implies that he believed that the value of money was not 'intrinsic'. In this regard, he appears an early advocate of the nominalist and social constructionist tradition in which money is a matter of law and convention; it does what we agree it should do (Schumpeter, 1994 [1954], 56). However, over the centuries, the Aristotelian version has had a greater – if indirect – influence via eighteenth- and nineteenth-century 'classical economics', in which the concepts of 'neutral' money, commodity money, and 'real' value were established.

Commodity Theory and 'Metallism'

Adam Smith's *The Wealth of Nations* (1776) followed Aristotle's derivation of money's origins and functions from assumptions about the nature of society and human motivation. Smith explained that the advantages of the division of labour increased production but removed self-sufficiency. Henceforth, specialized producers could only satisfy their wants by the barter exchange of their respective produce. Eventually, it was found that they could maximize their exchange opportunities by holding stocks of the most tradable commodities as media of exchange – iron nails and dried cod in Smith's account. In other words, money as a *medium of exchange* is the *commodity* that 'buys' all other commodities.

Although Smith's sternest critic, Karl Marx, saw the importance of the new forms of capitalist bank-credit paper money, which we shall discuss shortly, he also focused on commodity money. Marx's 'labour theory of value' – in which the value of commodities is determined by the labour time necessary for their production – led him to present a version of the commodity theory of money. The value of the labour involved in mining and minting gold is embodied in the coin. Therefore, the commodity gold can become the instrument for the measurement and exchange of other values in relation to 'the quantity of any other commodity in which the same amount of labour time is congealed' (Marx, 1976 [1867], 186; for a comprehensive orthodox Marxist analysis of money, see Lapavitsas, 2016). Nevertheless, Marx dismissed the 'classical economics' of Adam Smith and his early nineteenth-century followers for its inability to see that 'capital' was not simply the material means of production: technology and other physical resources. Rather, capital entailed a *social relation* between those who owned the material means of production – capitalist entrepreneurs – and those who operated them – the workers. However, Marx failed to apply the same analysis to money and fully to grasp that *all* money is credit in the sense that its value is given by the existence of debts that it can cancel (Ingham, 2004; 63–6; Smithin, 2018).

For 'classical economics', money is a spontaneous unintended consequence of what Smith called rational individuals' 'propensity to truck, barter, and exchange' in seeking to maximize self-interest. Their individual strategies culminate in the 'wisdom' of the market – the 'invisible hand'– which 'chooses' the most tradable commodity. Commodities are held in the first instance for their 'intrinsic' value and/or usefulness – Smith's nails and cod, or gold. However, as trade in some commodities increases, their potential is recognized, setting in train a momentum that culminates in the transition from barter to money as the most exchangeable commodity. This 'creation myth' was firmly established by the Cambridge economist William Stanley Jevons in his *Money and the Mechanism of Exchange* (1875): money emerges spontaneously to avoid the 'inconvenience' of the 'absence of a double coincidence of wants' in barter. This was illustrated with the example of how the naturalist Alfred Russel Wallace went hungry on an expedition to the Malay Peninsula in the 1850s because, although food was abundantly available, his party did not have any commodities that were acceptable at the time for which it could be bartered.

The development of coinage was easily explained by commodity-exchange theory with the further conjecture that precious metal commodities have the additional advantages of portability, divisibility, and durability, which enable the minting of commodity money into convenient uniform pieces of equal weight and fineness. Consequently, this theory of money is also known as 'metallism'. Endorsed by the leading constitutional scholar and philosopher John Locke during a dispute in the late seventeenth century, 'metallism' became the accepted basis for monetary practice and policy (see Martin, 2013, chap. 8). At that time, the price of silver on the European markets was greater than the London price offered by the mint for coinage. Consequently, silver was held as a non-monetary store of value and not taken to the mint for coinage. The London financier William Lowndes proposed a 20 per cent reduction of the silver content of English crowns

(5 shillings) to increase the nominal value of coins above the price of silver and so discourage the export of silver with a higher market price than its face value as coin. Locke dismissed the proposal for being based on a false theory of money. Silver, he argued in 1695, is the 'instrument and measure of commerce by its quantity, which is the measure also of its intrinsick value' (quoted in Martin, 2013, 126). He argued that measures of economic and physical phenomena should be constructed on the same principle: both values being measured were given in 'nature'. For Lowndes to claim that a coin would retain its value despite losing 20 per cent of its silver was as mistaken as lengthening a foot by dividing it into fifteen parts instead of twelve and calling them both inches (Martin, 2013, 127).

'Metallism' became closely related to economics' 'quantity theory' of money, in which price levels are determined by the exchange ratio of quantities of commodities: precious metal and goods. Using mathematics, the theory was formalized by Irving Fisher at the height of the gold standard era (Fisher 1911). In its simplest form, his equation holds that the price level (P) is a direct function of the quantity (M) and velocity (V) of circulation of money in relation to the number of transactions (T): that is, $MV = PT$. Although the equation is a logical identity in which each side equals the other, it was generally assumed that MV determines PT: that is, the quantity of money is the *causal* factor in price inflation. In chapter 4, we will see that 'quantity theory' lay behind the 'monetarist' attempts in the 1970s and 1980s to control inflation.

The Essentials of 'Classical' Theory: 'Neutral' Money and 'Real' Value

By the late nineteenth century, commodity-exchange theory – money's neutrality and the concept of the 'real' economy – was the accepted orthodoxy. As John Stuart Mill put it in his *Principles of Political Economy* (1871), money's existence 'does not interfere with the operation of any laws of value' (quoted in Ingham, 2004, 19); it enables us to do more efficiently what had been done before without it. As we outlined in chapter 1, value in this theory derives from the utility or functional contribution of factors of production, which is determined independently of the use of money. Money merely measures the value of the pre-existing 'real' values which exchange at ratios which express the relative contributions/ utility of 'real' factors of production. 'Capital' was seen in terms of the contribution of machinery, land and buildings, and other physical assets to production. Modern mainstream economics has continued to view capital in essentially the same way as 'stocks' of factors that can be expected to generate profits over time. As we have noted, this conception of capital was at odds with business usage. From Italy from the thirteenth century to Britain in the eighteenth, the word 'capital' was used mostly to refer to money advanced by owners or shareholders to establish a business, as it is by and large today by those who deal with balance sheets (Hodgson, 2015).

The theory of the 'real' economy reached its most refined expression in the 1870s in French economist Léon Walras's mathematical model of the market economy as a series of simultaneous equations with which he demonstrated the ultimate theoretical equilibrium (see Orléan, 2014b). At this equilibrium point, the twin forces of supply and demand have produced prices at which all demand has been satisfied and all supply is exhausted. But to solve the equations, Walras had to arbitrarily assign a numerical value to one of the commodities – the *numeraire* – enabling price formation but making no contribution to the value of commodities. Elaborated by Kenneth Arrow and Gérard Debreu in 1954 as 'general equilibrium theory', it became the cornerstone of prestigious mathematical economic theory. None the less, one of the theory's most eminent practitioners found it puzzling and disconcerting that 'the best model of the economy [Arrow–Debreu] cannot find room for . . . [money]' (Hahn, 1987, 1).

Coming to Terms with Modern Capitalist Money

Throughout history, everyday transactions had been mainly conducted with base metal and highly debased silver coins (Davies, 1996). Full-weight precious metal coins were used infrequently, and by the end of the nineteenth century, even in countries on the gold standard, they were only a very small part of the money supply, bearing little relationship to the vast increase in transactions. Paper banknotes circulated without being converted into the gold that they represented, and, as we shall see in chapter 4, capitalist enterprise was conducted with credit – 'promissory notes' and 'bills of exchange' (IOUs) – that could ultimately, but not necessarily, be redeemed in currency. In everyday life in politically stable countries, there was widespread, but objectively unwarranted, confidence that all these forms of money were backed by gold. But, of course, there simply wasn't enough to fulfil the promise to 'pay the bearer on demand' the sum of gold denominated on the banknote or to redeem the merchant's 'bill of exchange'.

As we have noted, these developments contradicted academic economics' fundamental explanatory tenet: rational maximization of self-interest by *homo economicus*. It was rational in the first instance to hold commodities that became media of exchange because they had 'intrinsic' value and/or 'utility': Smith's iron nails and dried cod served two purposes – *use-value* and *exchange-value*. But why, as the Austrian economist Carl Menger famously asked, should rational individuals be willing to exchange goods for 'little metal disks apparently useless as such, or for documents representing the latter' (Menger, 1892, 239). The question was an entirely unnecessary, self-inflicted consequence of the 'creation myth' of money's emergence from 'intrinsic' value or 'utility'. Striving to maintain the integrity of orthodoxy in the face of 'incompatible' credit theory's growing relevance in the era of non-commodity money, Menger simply reiterated the rational self-interest axiom. But it is a circular argument to say that individuals accept 'useless' discs and paper because they are advantageous media of exchange. As we noted in the previous chapter, it is advantageous for the rational individual only if all others do likewise, which cannot be explained by the same axiom. None the less, efforts were made to cling to the established academic orthodoxy, and Menger's restatement of it remains a canonical text for some schools of modern economics. We shall see, however, that money's introduction and acceptance require a different explanation.

One way to maintain the relevance of commodity/quantity theory was to insist on a sharp distinction between 'money' and 'credit', which was, in fact, increasingly blurred both in principle and in practice. As we shall see in chapter 4, 'promissory notes' and other forms of credit – that is, 'claims' to money – had circulated in late medieval commerce without being redeemed in precious metal currency. But by the nineteenth century, capitalism was based almost entirely on these means of payment. Joseph Schumpeter remarked that one could not ride a claim to a horse, but now one could pay with a claim to money (Schumpeter, 1994 [1954], 321). In another strategy, the concept of the *velocity* of money gained greater prominence in the commodity/quantity theory to explain the growing disparity between quantities of money and the number of goods and transactions. If the same quantity of money moved faster from hand to hand, this increase in velocity could finance more transactions. In his textbook *Money* (1928), reprinted many times over thirty years, the Cambridge economist Dennis Robertson illustrated the velocity of money with the story of Bob and Joe's journey to Derby Day at Epsom races to sell a barrel of beer (Robertson, 1948 [1928], 33). As the June day got hotter and the two men grew thirstier, Bob asked if he could buy a pint of Joe's share with his only 3 penny coin. Joe agreed, and soon after, to quench his own thirst, he bought a pint of Bob's share with the *same* 3 penny coin. Thirst and transactions continued until they arrived at Epsom with an empty barrel. Had the beer been sold at the races, they would made a good profit, but they were left with only one 3 penny coin, which was now back in Joe's pocket.

The story was intended to illustrate how economics explained the satisfaction of Bob and Joe's 'utilities' by the velocity of a single neutral medium of exchange – the relevance of the business failure was not mentioned. However, the story also exposes the vacuity of the concept of the 'velocity' of a 'quantity' of a physical medium of exchange. Schumpeter again quipped: money could have 'a velocity so great that it enables things to be in different places at the same time' (Schumpeter, 1994 [1954], 320). In fact, the parable of Bob and Joe could just as easily illustrate the alternative 'credit' theory of money. They didn't need to *exchange* a coin for beer to meet their needs. Using *money of account*, they could have recorded the credit and debit transactions, to be settled later if they had consumed different amounts of beer.

Despite technological changes in forms of transmitting money – from coins handed over in exchange to electronic impulses travelling through cyberspace – the concepts 'quantity' and 'velocity' continue to inform the analysis of money in many modern economics textbooks (for example, Mankiw and Taylor, 2008). To Robertson and many others, these concepts appeared appropriate for circulating coinage; but do they make sense of electronic credit-transmitting impulses passing through cyberspace? We will pursue this question shortly in the discussion of the 'credit' and 'state' theories of money and again in chapter 4; but first we should note the most important flaws in commodity-exchange theory.

Commodity-Exchange Theory: History and Logic

In the absence of an historical record of money's emergence from barter, the late nineteenth-century commodity-exchange theorists correctly pointed out that we could only rely on a conjectural account of money's 'logical' origins. This was derived from the conception of society as a web of economic exchanges driven by individual utility-maximization. Repeated over the years in textbooks, 'conjecture' became 'fact'; but there is no historical evidence that barter was ever the most prevalent means for the exchange of goods and that money evolved spontaneously to remedy its inefficiencies (see Graeber, 2011). Before markets with money prices, the distribution of goods in society was governed either by norms of reciprocity – for example, allocation according to age, sex, and status in tribal or clan society; or by rationed distribution controlled by centralized command systems such as in ancient Egypt (Polanyi et al., 1957).

Chapter 1 introduced a distinction between two functions of money – *medium of exchange* and *means of payment* – which has not been generally observed since they were conflated in Walker's list. Following Grierson and Keynes, it was argued that the function of *money of account/measure/ standard of value* was the key to the distinction. *Means of payment* are the credits that can settle the debt incurred in a purchase or a loan because credit and debt are denominated in the same *money of account*. Commodities priced in money of account are the signals to which myriad unconnected individuals can respond anonymously in large multilateral markets. (Recall that to solve the equations in his mathematical model of market equilibrium, Walras had arbitrarily to assign a constant value [*numeraire*] to one of the commodities which could act as a money of account.) However, in 'real' barter, it is implausible that bilateral bargaining, based on the individual traders' preferences, could lead to the emergence of a universal money of account. In barter, the ratios (relative values) of commodities would be specific to each exchange. The ratio of, say, ducks and chickens will vary from trade to trade: that is, ducks and chickens do not have a market 'price' denominated in money of account. Rather, bartered commodities have countless different exchange ratios; 100 goods could yield 4,950 exchange ratios (Davies, 1996, 15). The theory of the barter origins of commodity money maintains that constant 'higgling and haggling' transforms the numerous potential barter exchange ratios into a market 'price'. But, '[t]here are as many valuations as there are goods and circumstances of exchange, with no possibility of being able to deduce anything whatever from them' (Orléan, 2014a, 127). We shall see that an important 'incompatibility' of the alternative credit theory is the reversal of the causal link between money and the market. Commodity theory contends that money of account emerges from 'higgling and haggling' in barter, whereas, for credit theory, genuine markets in which price signals are posted *presuppose* the existence of money of account (Ingham, 2004; Orléan 2014a, 2014b).

None the less, R.A. Radford's (1945) personal account of the use of cigarettes as media of exchange in a POW camp in the Second World War has been widely used in economics textbooks as an example of the spontaneous emergence of commodity money (for example, Mankiw and Taylor, 2008, 126). To be sure, cigarettes were used in exchange, but, as to be expected in the transit camps, the barter exchange ratio of cigarettes varied widely. A more stable cigarette standard did occur in the atypical conditions of the permanent camps: small-scale, repeated exchanges between a stable population of 'traders' who were known to each other. More importantly, 'the highest level of commercial organisation' in camp shops, 'controlled by representatives of the Senior British Officer', prohibited barter, posted price lists, and accepted only cigarettes as payment. Eventually, a camp paper currency ('Bully Mark'), backed by a fixed exchange rate with food ('bully'), was organized by the shops (Radford, 1945, 192, 197–8). In other words, the camp monetary system was based on the officers' authority and control of the shops: that is, it did not emerge spontaneously and exclusively from individuals engaged in barter.

Credit and State Theories of Money

The 'credit theory' of money, 'monetary nominalism', and the 'state theory' of money have elements in common in their opposition to commodity theory.

Nominalism and Credit Money

The departure from 'classical' orthodox monetary theory in the first sentence of Keynes's *A Treatise on Money* (1930) provides an answer to our earlier query about the relative importance of the functions in Walker's list: 'Money of Account, namely that in which Debts and Prices and General Purchasing Power are expressed, is the *primary concept* of a Theory of Money" (Keynes, 1930, 3, emphasis added). Keynes continues with a distinction between money and media of exchange. Money of account defines 'money proper', which, consequently, can settle debt because both are denominated in the same unit. Money 'proper' is to be distinguished from 'something which is merely used as a convenient medium of exchange on the spot . . . which may approach to being Money. . . . But if this is all, we have scarcely emerged from the stage of Barter. Money proper in the full sense of the term *can only exist* in relation to money of account' (Keynes, 1930, 3 emphasis added). In other words, Keynes offers a nominalist conception of money as something 'which answers the description' of money rather than being an exchangeable commodity.

His ideas had germinated during the early 1920s in research on money, weights, and measures in the ancient Near East, referred to as his 'Babylonian madness' in a letter to his fiancée Lydia Lopokova (Ingham, 2004). Over 5,000 years ago, these bureaucratic states did not issue currency but used units of account to measure the value of stocks of commodities; to denominate taxes and loans; and to set wages and rents. Credits and debits, recorded in cuneiform on clay tablets, were netted out and any outstanding debt was paid in barley or silver by weight. The debts were denominated in the money of account/standard of value comprising a fixed ratio of quantities of barley (*gur*) and silver by weight (*shekel*).

Critics of the nominalist theory that 'moneyness' is assigned by money of account have taken the existence of barley and silver in Babylon as evidence of the material commodity origins of money (Lapavitsas, 2005; and the reply in Ingham, 2006). However, the money of account was not merely barley or silver as material things, but an *invariant value ratio* between the two: that is, an *abstraction* produced by human consciousness ('existing in thought rather than matter', *Concise Oxford English Dictionary*). Moreover, the barley side of the ratio was also an abstraction: the notional quantity required to feed a family for a month.

Unlike phenomena whose functions follow from their material properties – for example, glass and windows – it is necessary *intentionally* to assign money's functions (Searle, 1995). If a nominal value is assigned and accepted, anything can serve as the token credit to bear and transmit it. Contrary to commodity theory, the assigning of a nominal value (money of account) is accomplished not in the process of exchange but by the authority of the state or community (Keynes, 1930, 3). The repeated objection that the value of money cannot be intentionally assigned is based on one or other of two misconceptions of money's value. The first follows from the assumption that money must have 'intrinsic' value for it to be held as a medium of exchange – Menger's problem of 'useless' discs and paper. The second is that money measures and represents the *pre-existing* values that are generated by the material factors in the 'real' economy. Max Weber's conception of money as a 'weapon' can be used to elaborate an implication of 'credit theory' and to clarify the difficulties (Ingham, 2019). 'Useless' discs and paper are *nominal* but *prospective* values with which *actual substantive* values (prices) are produced in the struggles between possessors of the *nominal prospective* 'credits' and possessors of goods. 'Purchasing power' is not 'possessed' by money but is produced in a social and economic relation in which 'sale and purchase is the exchange of a commodity for credit' (Mitchell Innes, 1914, 355).

'Imaginary Money' and Promises to Pay

The explanatory value of monetary nominalism and credit theory can be shown in the analysis of two critical developments in medieval European money which presaged modern capitalism. First, Charlemagne's (c. 742–814) attempt to unify the monetary fragmentation of the Holy Roman Empire led to what the great French historian Marc Bloch called the '*décrochement*' (de-linking) of money of account and coined currency (Bloch, 1954 [1936]). Second, the circulation of private credits, or promises to pay (IOUs), became widely used as payment in merchant networks. Both examples illustrate Keynes's astute observation that if the same 'thing' always answered the same 'description' of money, then the distinction between money as *money of account* and a money thing that is a *means of payment* would not be significant (Keynes 1930, 3).

To bring coherence to the large number of mints and coinages which had sprung up after the collapse of the Roman empire, Charlemagne imposed a single money of account of a pound weight of silver divided into 20 shillings and 240 pennies. All three were used for the denomination of debts and prices, but pound and shilling silver coins were not minted. Pounds and shillings were *nominal values* and the *coinage* consisted of silver pennies. All the diverse existing coins were to become commensurable by having an exchange rate with the new money of account. There were two significant consequences. First, unminted units of account encouraged a conception of money as an abstract rather than a material intrinsic value – 'imaginary' or 'ghost' money entered European consciousness (Einaudi, 1936; Fantacci,

2008). Second, the separation of money's two components – nominal unit of value and material precious metal coinage – gave rulers an additional way to advantageously manipulate the value of money and use it as a 'weapon'.

Monarchs were adept at increasing their spending power by debasement: reducing precious metal content to produce more coins of the same nominal value. The de-linking of actual coins and money of account gave them a much easier way to profit from their monetary power. Monarchs could now replace their unminted virtual, or 'imaginary', coin, used as money of account for denominating tax debts, with another one that was nominally valued to be worth more of the coins in circulation. For example, in the fourteenth century, Charles VI of France replaced the 'imaginary' cheval à franc, nominally valued at 20 circulating sous coins, with an écu à la couronne worth 22 sous. Wealthy aristocratic and ecclesiastical landowners were disadvantaged as it now required more circulating coins to discharge tax debts denominated in the revised money of account. They commissioned Nicolas Oresme, Grand Master of the College of Navarre in Paris, to address the problem and to recommend an acceptable monetary policy (the following account is from Martin, 2013, 91–5). Oresme's *A Treatise on the Origin, Nature, Law, and Alterations of Money* (1360) challenged the medieval idea of absolute and divinely sanctioned royal power. As Aristotle had similarly argued, Oresme insisted that money was an instrument for the mutual benefit of all and should not be controlled and used to the advantage of any interest.

Oresme's analysis inadvertently revealed the unresolved dilemmas and contradictions that remain at the heart of monetary power and policy to the present day. One solution to France's problems would have been to negotiate a ratio between a money of account and a quantity of precious metal fixed in a standard coin at a value acceptable to all interests: creditors, debtors, the wealthy, and the king. But, of course, the dispute itself was evidence that there was no such consensual interest. And how could any standard be enforced if it were not in the interest of the sovereign to do so? Moreover, Oresme noted that a rigidly fixed precious metal standard might not be able to meet the demand for currency in an expanding economy – as later monetary authorities came to realize. On the other hand, it was unthinkable that the sovereign's right to issue coin could be challenged. None the less, Oresme declared that if the monarch could not be trusted, then the 'community alone has the right to decide' on the supply and nominal value of money. But, of course, the idea of a 'community' with a single interest was a fiction; in an unequal society, alterations in the value of money affected classes and interests differently – especially debtors and creditors.

The late medieval European 'commercial revolution' led to the increased use of promissory notes, or bills of exchange, among merchants in lieu of direct payment. Such acknowledgements of personal debt (IOUs) had been used for millennia alongside coined currency. But in medieval Europe they gradually became *transferable* (*negotiable*): that is, an acknowledgement of debt (IOU) issued by a person of known wealth to his creditor was accepted by a third party in the expectation that it could be passed on as payment to someone else. A's signed note (IOU) held by B as a promise of A's future payment might be accepted by C as an acknowledgement of a debt owed to him by B and thence might be transferred by D, E, and so on. Any acceptor of the IOU had a 'claim' on issuer A that the debt would be settled currency; but in some commercial networks, the chain of acceptances could be very extensive.

By the sixteenth century, bills and promissory notes were widely established in law as a contract of payment which was legally transferable beyond the original signatories. This opened the way for the banknotes which were issued as the legal liability of the issuing bank (Ingham, 2004,121–4). As we shall see, states also became issuers of IOUs as payment for goods and services which were redeemed, in turn, by their acceptance as payment of taxes imposed by the state. Both developments replaced the fragile *personal* trust in the IOUs, based on the viability of the merchants in the networks, with *impersonal* trust in the issuing bank and state authority.

Money: 'Real' or 'Imaginary'?

Like the de-linking of the money account and coined currency, the circulation of bills and notes had an impact on the conception of money. If *accepting* a promise was all that was necessary for it to function as money, was *all* money a 'claim' on goods or a 'credit' that could settle a debt? Was money an *abstract* rather than *material* force? 'Credit gives Motion, yet it cannot be said to exist . . . it is the essential Shadow of Something that it is Not', Daniel Defoe pondered in 1710 (cited in Ingham, 2004, 41). In a penetrating anticipation of later thinking, Sir James Stueart (1767) not only made a distinction between 'money coin' and 'money of accompt', but also inverted the logic of the commodity theory of money: money is that 'which purely in itself is of no material use to man but which acquires such an estimation from his opinion of it as to become the universal measure of what is called value' (quoted in Schumpeter, 1994 [1954], 297). The 'reality' of material money was ultimately dependent on acceptance of the 'imaginary'. Despite the official 'metallist' doctrine and the existence of precious metal coinage, notes and bills had become a large indispensable part of the money supply by the late eighteenth century. As we have noted, however, commodity theory sidestepped the contradiction by holding to a distinction between 'money' and 'credit' that is still widely accepted in modern economics.

The intellectual dispute was sharpened by the Bank of England's suspension of note convertibility into gold during the Napoleonic Wars (1797). The economy continued to operate as before, adding support to the view that 'intrinsically' precious metal was not necessary for the functions and value of money. Capitalist entrepreneurs saw the advantages of a flexible supply of money no longer constrained by convertibility. Typically, the most powerful governing class of wealthy creditors and landowners defended 'sound' gold-backed money, which was reinstated after the war. The government's return to 'metallist' policy was supported by a body of opinion known as the 'Currency School', including the eminent economist David Ricardo. But in an early expression of industrial capitalist interests, the establishment's position was confronted by coherent opposition. The 'Banking School' advocated a more flexible monetary policy, based on credit money, that could respond to the need to stimulate production and consumption. The Birmingham capitalist banker and Member of Parliament Thomas Attwood advocated a proto-Keynesian prescription that the supply of credit should be allowed to increase to the point at which 'the general demand for labour, in all the great departments of industry, becomes greater than its supply' (quoted in Ingham, 2004, 108). Members of the Banking School advanced a 'credit theory' of money: a monetary transaction was not an *exchange* of commodities – precious metal for goods; but, rather, the *settlement of the debt* with a credit. 'The real question then to be considered is not whether this or that particular form of credit be entitled to the designation of "money", but whether, without a perversion of terms and an outrage of principle, that denomination can be applied to credit in any shape' (John Fullarton, cited in Ingham, 2004, 42).

Two intertwined meanings of *neutral* money are evident in Ricardo's support for the Currency School concept of *natural* metallic money: '[W]ithout a standard [money] would be exposed to all the fluctuations to which the *ignorance* and *interests* of the issuers might subject it . . . there can be no unerring measure of either length, of weight, of time, or of *value* unless there be some *object in nature* to which the standard itself can be referred' (Ricardo, quoted in Ingham, 2004, 15, emphasis added). If money were a 'neutral' measure of values produced in the 'real' economy, it followed that it was 'neutral' in the sense that it *should* not be controlled by any interest because, in the final analysis, it *could* not be effectively controlled. As only 'real' factors of production create wealth, the 'illusionary' bank credit money would eventually lead to an oversupply and inevitable inflation.

These antithetical theoretical positions persisted without resolution because they represented two opposed economic interests in which money was a 'weapon'. Flexible bank credit money for production and consumption conflicted with creditors' demands for 'sound money' to prevent an inflationary erosion of the value of their wealth. We shall see that matters came to a head a century later in the 1930s with Keynes's rejection of the 'barbarous relic' of the gold standard and his reiteration of the view that money was essentially a public utility to be used for the common good.

The State Theory of Money

There is a long tradition in which money is understood as a legal construct, devised and enforced by the state. During the late seventeenth century, opponents of John Locke's 'metallism', such as Nicholas Barbon, argued that all money, including coinage, was legally established credit (for an account of money and law, see Desan, 2014, chapters 7, 8, and 9; Fox and Ernst, 2016).

However, the recent revival of state theory follows Georg Knapp's *State Theory of Money*, which arose in the context of the politics of creating the unified German state in the nineteenth century. In his polemical retort to those who believed that economic market exchange was a reliable foundation for stable money and stable social order, Knapp thought it 'absurd to understand money without the idea of the state' (1973 [1905], vii–viii).

The establishment of both a monopoly of coercion in territorial space and a monetary space, based on control of the money of account, occurred concurrently as essential elements of state formation. The unit of account and the form of money declared by the state for denominating and settling debts owed by the state to suppliers and employees is, in turn, the only one which the state will accept as payment of the taxes that it imposes. Following Knapp's use of the Latin word *charta* (token) for the definition of money as a *chartal* means of payment, the 'state theory' of money is also known as 'chartalism'. The state need not be the only issuer of money, but Knapp argued that privately issued banknotes only become valid money (*valuata* money) if they are denominated in the state's money of account and accepted in payment of debts owed to the state. (Today, taxes are paid by the electronic transfer of money from private bank deposits denominated in the state's money of account.)

Keynes's *The General Theory of Employment, Interest and Money* was strongly influenced by Knapp's state theory, which he combined with the 'credit theory' of the 'brave army of heretics' from the Banking School. This challenged the Ricardian 'classical' orthodoxy, which 'had conquered England as completely as the Holy Inquisition had conquered Spain' (Keynes, 1973 [1936], 32–3, 370–1). It was, Keynes believed, 'something of a curiosity and a mystery' that 'classical' economics 'had reached conclusions quite different from what the ordinary uninstructed person would expect'. But with typical lucidity that resonates to this day, he saw that the 'logical beauty of classical economics [which] could explain much social injustice and apparent cruelty . . . afforded a measure of justification to the free activities of the individual capitalist, attracted it to the support of the dominant social force behind authority' (Keynes 1997 [1936], 33). Keynes believed that his orthodox colleagues and politicians were theoretically oblivious to the 'outstanding problem' of unemployment caused by deficient effective demand (for a clear, concise account, see Skidelsky, 2018).

During the political and economic crises of the inter-war years, the major countries were unable to maintain the gold standard; they had insufficient gold confidently to promise and to be believed that their currency was backed by gold. In the absence of this self-imposed constraint on the money supply, governments were free to follow Keynes by increasing their expenditure if private investment in production were insufficient to create full employment and income for consumption. The state should make good the shortfall with expenditure to bring 'aggregate demand' to the necessary level to stimulate production. Monetary orthodoxy agreed that government spending could be effective as a short-term measure but continued to insist that this would inevitably lead to inflation in the long run.

Similar prescriptions were put forward elsewhere in the mid-twentieth century: for example, Abba Lerner's 'functional finance' in the USA, which argued that the level of government spending should be set at a level which enables the purchase of all goods that it is possible to produce at a given time (Lerner, 1943, 39). Following Lerner, Knapp, Keynes, and the earlier 'credit' theorists, Randall Wray and associates in the USA have produced Modern Monetary Theory (MMT) (Wray, 2012). Its main thrust is directed against what they believe are the erroneous assumptions and implications in the mainstream economic theory which currently frames government monetary and fiscal policy. First, MMT points out that state spending does not depend on the *prior* collection of taxes on private incomes. Unless a state itself imposes a restriction on the issue of its own money – for example, with a gold standard – it can never be without the money to finance its expenditure (Wray, 2012). As the modern state creates money by 'fiat' – the tap on the computer key – it does not require our money in taxes *before* it spends. Rather, we require the state's money to meet our tax debts, and, in effect, taxation is a means of withdrawing inflationary potential from the economy.

If the state does not adopt self-imposed restrictions such as a gold standard on the supply of money, MMT contends that the state – as the sovereign money power – can simply spend money into existence. Consequently, there is no *technical* monetary reason why it cannot do so to the limit of full employment. MMT has yet to have a significant impact on mainstream academic economics, but it has triggered an increasingly wide-ranging debate in the USA (see the exchanges at *www.neweconomicperspectives.org*) and in Europe (*www.sovereignmoney.eu*). As a 'myth buster', MMT has exposed flaws in the conventional account of the nature of money; its creation; and current fiscal and monetary arrangements and policy. However, how and how much money is produced is ultimately a political matter, not one of technical economics. We will see in chapters 4 and 5 that today's institutions for the creation of money are the result of struggles and political conflict over the centuries between states, capitalist financiers, and taxpayers. In chapter 7, we will return to the question of whether this monetary system, wrought by the conflicts, represents the gradual evolution of technically efficient 'best practice' or whether the historical developments have produced a workable but none the less inherently flawed outcome.

State theory provides answers to the two questions that are not dealt with satisfactorily by commodity-exchange theory. First, states have been the most effective authority for the creation of the nominal unit of account by which money is distinguished from exchangeable commodities with many fluctuating exchange rates. Second, by spending money into existence and demanding its return in taxes, states provide a compelling basis for the acceptance of money without recourse to Menger's tautology that it is rational to do so if all others do likewise. Furthermore, the value of taxes gives value to money. Sociologists have emphasized the importance of trust for the acceptance of money, but this needs to be more precisely specified. The acceptability, or trustworthiness, of money does not depend in the first instance on the transacting individuals' *personal* trust. Rather, the wide acceptance of money is based on the issuer's promise to accept it in payment of any debt owed, which shifts the burden of trust from the transacting individuals to the issuer, creating *impersonal* trust and – it must not be forgotten – a degree of *compulsion*.

The legal 'Case of Mixt Monies' in early seventeenth-century England (Gilbert *v.* Brett, 1604) nicely illustrates how – as Keynes explained – states write the monetary 'dictionary' by declaring what 'describes' money: that is, the money of account for the denomination of debts and prices. The case arose out of Elizabeth I's debasement of the Irish currency in 1601. Brett had purchased £200 of goods from a London merchant, Gilbert, and proffered payment which included some Irish coins which now contained less silver than English coins of the same nominal value – hence 'mixt monies'. Gilbert refused to accept the payment and the case was referred for a ruling by the Chief Judges of the Queen's Privy Council. They found in favour of Brett, establishing in common law that debts were obligations valued at the time of the contract in the *abstract* monetary units that the sovereign declared, not by any variation in the precious metal content of the actual means of payment (Fox, 2011).

State theory has been widely misunderstood. First, the existence of private credit money and, as we shall, 'complementary' local community currencies (see chapter 6) is taken as evidence that the state is not necessary for the creation of money. We will return to this question in the following chapter, but some points of clarification should be noted. As I have explained, the declaration and enforcement of a money of account for the denomination of prices and debts requires an *authority* – it does not emerge spontaneously from the interaction of self-interested individuals. The authority need not be a state: for example, sixteenth-century Europe's mercantile financial networks used their own private unit of account, as did the officers in the POW camp. Moreover, many of the local community currencies and the capitalist financial networks' IOUs, which are held to counter state theory, are denominated in their host state's unit of account: that is, they 'shadow' the dollar, euro, and so on. Furthermore, these non-state moneys are directly embedded in the financial networks, dependent on the creditworthiness of the participants; consequently, they are notoriously unstable. Of course, some states fall into this category, but successful states have produced the most stable and enduring money.

Preoccupied with the 'real', or non-monetary, theory of economic value, mainstream economics has placed state theory's adherents among the monetary 'cranks', ridiculed for thinking that the state rather than the market economy can create value. Weber's distinction between *formal* and *substantive* validity of money helps to clarify the issue (Ingham, 2019). States cannot *directly* determine the *substantive* validity of money: that is, its purchasing power at any point in time. But they can declare and impose its *formal* validity: that is, what is accepted as valid payment for debts, as the Privy Council did in 1604. Formally *valid prospective* value is wielded as a 'weapon' in the struggles that determine *actual substantive* values. Furthermore, the existence of enforceable tax debts further anchors *both* money's *formal validity* and *substantive value*. States are simultaneously the largest makers and receivers of payments. It is a mark of a strong and successful state to be able to impose its money as a means of payment for the goods and services that it purchases and to insist that it is the only money accepted as tax payment. Conversely, the inability to impose and collect taxes in its declared money is both a cause and consequence of state weakness – as shown by the experience of Russia and Argentina (Woodruff, 1999; Ingham, 2004; Saiag, 2019).

'A Steadfast Refusal to Face Facts'?

In the face of the logical flaws, historical inaccuracies, and a well-established – if shunned – alternative, how have the irreconcilable theories co-existed for so long? Why has 'neutral' money and associated assumptions endured in mainstream economic theory and practice? It is as if the Copernican revolution had not been able entirely to displace Ptolemy's 'geocentric' theory of the sun's rotation around the earth. According to one of its most eminent – but critical – practitioners, orthodox monetary economics shows 'a steadfast refusal to face facts', remaining beset by 'continuing muddles' (Goodhart, 2009). It persists with the assumptions of 'neutral' money and the corollary that economic value is produced by 'real' forces, independently of the existence of money, as it would in barter (see, for example, Mankiw and Taylor, 2008, chap. 4). To repeat: this is not merely an 'academic' question – theories of money are an inextricable part of the 'struggle for economic existence'. Two examples of the political, practical, and ideological consequences of the 'neutral' money concept will be discussed later: the economic rationale for the creation of a European common currency (chapter 5); and the inability of mainstream macroeconomic models to account for the possibility – indeed, probability – of financial crises (chapter 7).

Conclusion

In the final analysis, the incompatibility of the theories of money is to be found in the different underlying theories, or 'visions', of society on which they are implicitly based. The strong implication of most mainstream economics – at least that which derives from the conventional interpretation of Adam Smith – is that social order is created spontaneously by individuals in pursuit of their self-interest. Society based on a division of labour is held together by webs of advantaged economic interdependence. Altruism, fellow-feeling, and pride in work exist but they are not the *primary* motivation for the baker's provision of wholesome bread – she just wants us to return the next day. Using a similar conception of society, Friedrich Hayek argued that the state monopoly of money should be replaced by myriad freely competing currencies from which rational individuals would be able to select the most stable (Hayek, 1976). In effect, his hypothesis has been tested and found wanting by the proliferation of crypto-currencies such as Bitcoin – they have been disabled from performing money's functions by their chaotically fluctuating exchange-values. It is this anarchy of the market that Keynes had in mind in his comment that Hayek's economic theory, based exclusively on individual rationality and market competition, was 'an extraordinary example of how starting with a mistake, a remorseless logician can end in Bedlam' (Keynes, 1931, 394).

Two other general conceptions of social order underlie, respectively, the credit and state theories. On the one hand, credit theory's focus on money transactions as credit–debt relations points to their essential social dimension; trust in money derives from conventions and beliefs that also foster social order, as expounded in Émile Durkheim's sociology. On the other hand, state theory reminds us that the avoidance of Thomas Hobbes's 'war of all against all' requires submission to the coercive force of a 'Leviathan'. All three forms of order are found in varying degrees in viable societies and consequently in their monetary system.

3
A Social Theory of Money and Monetary Systems

Digital impulses transmitted electronically by cards, phones, and other devices are rapidly replacing banknotes, coins, and paper cheques; it appears that money has become 'virtual'. However, the widely held assumption that these technological changes will radically transform money is mistaken. There could be significant consequences: for example, control of the money supply might be enhanced if cash were replaced by digital money, enabling all citizens to have an account at the central bank (see chapter 7). But the fundamental nature of money will remain unchanged.

Money is and has always been virtual; it is in the category of socially constructed abstract – that is, non-material – powers that are actualized by social institutions. In *The Philosophy of Money*, Georg Simmel tells us that money is 'the value of things without the things themselves . . . the purest reification of means, a concrete instrument which is absolutely identical with its abstract concept' (Simmel, 1978 [1907], 121, 211). And as we noted in chapter 1, Alfred Mitchell Innes audaciously declared that the eye had never seen, nor the hand touched, a dollar – only the immaterial *promise* to pay a debt for a dollar.

The ingrained conception of money as a material 'thing' lies behind the conclusion that changes in the form of money – from analogue to digital – are significant. However, the legacy of commodity theory and metallism's misunderstanding of money should now be laid to rest. Any 'intrinsic' value of precious metal coins, or the convertibility of paper currency, was merely one of the ways of establishing the stability and acceptance of the means of payment. For the currency to be 'as good as gold' required the issuer's promise to maintain the price of precious metal and its link to the money of account: that is, the 'face value' of coins. In the UK's gold standard, for example, gold coins and the convertible paper notes were both manifestations of the same virtual pound sterling. Precious and base metal coins, paper, and traces of electronic impulses are all means of transmitting money: that is, means of payment denominated in money of account. As Philip Grierson tell us in his *Origins of Money*, 'money lies behind coin' (Grierson, 1977, 12).

Seen in this way, the old analogy of 'things' – coins and notes – 'circulating' with varying 'velocity', like blood through the body, is inappropriate. Rather, money should be understood in terms of a vast network of overlapping binary debt contracts which are settled by the transmission of reusable credits. Some time ago, I would ask my students if a hoard of Roman coins discovered in a Suffolk field by a metal detectorist were money. Pedantically, I said that the coins ceased to be money after the collapse of Rome and the disappearance of tax debts. The empire's provinces no longer 'had to export goods to the centre in order to buy back the money with which to pay the taxes' (Hopkins, 1978, 94).

Only at a superficial level, and not in every instance, does the act of settling a debt with money appear to involve the *exchange* of 'things'; rather, the 'things' bear and transmit credits to settle debt. Money is to be distinguished from *exchangeable commodities*. Payment made *in kind* – that is, with commodities – which occurs owing to a shortage or unacceptability of currency is widely misunderstood as a return to barter. For example, after the fall of Soviet communism in the 1990s, Russian power companies accepted paint in payment for electricity. However, as the debt for electricity was denominated in the rouble unit of account, it remained a monetary – not a barter – transaction. In this instance, paint was a money 'surrogate' (Woodruff, 2013), accepted as the thing that in Keynes's terms answered the 'description' of money (Keynes 1930, 4; see chapter 6).

Money's purchasing and debt-settling power exists only in virtue of the existence of actual and potential debts, denominated in the same money of account, awaiting settlement – or not, as in the case of the ditched Roman coins. Credit should not be understood only in the conventional sense as deferred payment – purchasing something 'on credit'. Rather, all three typical monetary transactions – *deferred payment, payment in advance,* and *payment 'on the spot'* – are debt contracts: that is, immediate cash payment is the settlement of a very short-term debt (Hicks, 1989, 41). The essential element in a monetary transaction is not the handing over of one thing in *exchange* for another, but, rather, the settlement of a debt incurred by a purchase or by the receipt of a loan. The nature of a 'spot' debt transaction is seen more clearly with a debit/credit card, which, unlike the coin or note, is handed back once it has transmitted its quantum of abstract value (credit). A debit card's transmission and cash both deliver credits which are then transmitted again and again by the same or different means in subsequent transactions to myriad holders.

The heterodox economist Hyman Minsky famously said that anyone could issue 'money' – the problem was getting it accepted (Minsky, 2008 [1986]). He was emphasizing that 'money' was 'credit' – an acknowledgement of debt, an IOU; but what he should have said is that anyone could issue 'credit' – the problem was getting it accepted as 'money'. All money is credit, but not all credit is money. The social relations and institutions that constitute a *monetary system* and a *monetary space* enable the transformation of 'credit' into money – a universally accepted final means of payment. We might think in terms of a hypothetical continuum at one end of which everyone offers their personal IOUs in payment – a situation not unlike Hayek's model of competing currencies. At the other end is the 'ideal' monetary system comprising two fundamental and related elements: first, a money of account which defines the abstract monetary value; and, second, forms and means of transmission of the abstract prospective value with which actual substantive values are established. Both elements are produced and maintained by institutions and social relations that determine their acceptability.

Empirically, societies rarely approximate this 'ideal'. There were multiple moneys of account within and across jurisdictions in medieval Europe and elsewhere, but they were gradually eliminated as monetary sovereignty was consolidated (Fantacci, 2008). Today, the existence of multiple moneys of account usually indicates a weak or disintegrating authority; but the existence of a variety of forms and means of transmission is commonplace – coins, cards, cheques, and so on. As Keynes understood, the things that 'answer' the money of account's 'description' of money can vary and, more importantly, their degree of acceptability can also vary: for example, the paint in Russia. Most monetary systems comprise a loose and shifting hierarchy of forms of money ranked by their acceptability (Bell, 2001). Where there is a single dominant issuer, the acceptability of various other forms is determined by the ease with which they are convertible into the money at the top of the hierarchy: that is, the final means of payment. For example, in modern capitalism, bank deposits comprise privately issued means of payment which are readily convertible into state-issued, publicly accepted cash. As we shall see in chapter 6, multiple 'complementary' moneys can co-exist in harmony, but they can also create monetary anarchy.

However, a cheque, denominated in the dominant money of account, drawn on a private deposit, might not be accepted without additional assurance of convertibility. Similarly, transmission of money by credit card is enhanced by the issuer's promise to assume liability for any loss incurred by the user. Credit cards are frequently used by economists to distinguish 'credit' and 'money' on the grounds that the use of credit card defers payment for the user. Furthermore, in this view, debit cards and cheques are not 'money', but a means of transmitting the 'money' which is 'contained' in bank accounts. Currency – cash and notes – and bank deposits are really money (Mankiw and Taylor, 2017, 196). However, as the reader will appreciate, this can become very confusing! The categorical distinction between 'money' and 'credit' becomes entangled with the further unclear distinction between 'money' – as abstract prospective value – and the means of its transmission. First, the credit card allows deferred payment for the user, but it does *immediately* transmit 'money' from the credit card company's account into the vendor's account. Second, the idea that notes, cash, and bank deposits 'contain' money is a confused vestige of the conception of money as things 'containing' intrinsic value. Bank deposits record the existences of credits of abstract value that can be transmitted in a variety of ways, one of which might be the 'portable credit' of coins and notes. To repeat, *the value of the credit that we know as 'money' is given by the existence of actual or prospective debts awaiting settlement.*

In practical terms, the fact that currency – notes and coins – is now an insignificant means of transmitting money caused enormous problems for attempts to measure and control the money supply with 'monetarism' in the 1980s (see chapter 4). What should be included in the measure of the money supply to be controlled? Notes and coins were M0, to which were added various kinds of bank deposits and financial assets from M1, M2, M3, M4, and so on. The conceptual difficulty – if not the practical measurement problem – of making a categorical distinction between money and *non*-money (credit) is overcome by referring to a hierarchy of forms of credit ranked in terms of their acceptability as payment of debt. In turn, acceptability is dependent on the credibility of the issuer's promise to accept their credit in payment for any debt.

We have argued that the denomination of abstract value (money of account) and the acceptability of forms/means of its transmission cannot be explained in terms of their utility/advantage for the individual. It is not self-evident that money will perform its economic functions effectively over an uncertain future. As Simmel explained, in monetary relations, unlike bilateral barter and the issue of personal acknowledgements of debt (IOU), 'a third factor is introduced between the two parties: the community . . . that accepts the money. . . . The liquidation of every private liability by money means that the community now assumes this obligation towards the creditor' (Simmel, 1978 [1907], 177).

This third factor is the authority that the monetary system exercises over all participants. We shall see in chapter 6 that this may be in actual 'communities' which support 'local exchange trading schemes' or other 'complementary' currencies that are found in many modern economies. Or the authority might be exercised by a network of merchants – as in seventeenth-century Europe. However, the most stable form of authoritative social order and consequently also of money is based on monopoly of the legitimate use of force with a territory: that is, the coercion and consent found in successful states. In establishing their monetary sovereignty, states have imposed severe physical penalties for debt, forgery, and counterfeiting, as Carl Wennerlind has shown in his *Casualties of Credit* (2011).

Consent and coercion also underpin the economic links between the state and society. As the largest makers and receivers of payments (tax revenue), states are the single most important economic agent in modern society, which ensures that their money is in most demand. Ultimately, however, greater stability of both the state and its money is achieved when 'might' is transformed into 'right': that is, when states and the monetary system are viewed as legitimate.

Legitimacy – that is, willing acceptance of the values of and justifications for the state's right to exercise powers contained in convention, law, and the constitution – is arguably the core strength of states and by implication their monetary system. At a still deeper level, state legitimacy might be fused with *hegemony* – the term used by the Marxist Antonio Gramsci to describe domination based on and, importantly, masked by an unquestioned acceptance of the normality and inevitability of the status quo of everyday life. And, of course, this is precisely what powerful controllers and producers of money have led us to believe. The hegemony of money is established when its 'intrinsic' value is deemed to exist in a natural realm beyond our control or in the reality of objective needs of the economy which are only open to interpretation by experts in economic science. It is here that the mysteries of monetary theory play a most essential role in preserving the social order. As Henry Ford Sr was said to have put it: 'It is well enough that the people of the Nation do not understand our banking and monetary system, for if they did, I believe that there would be a revolution before tomorrow morning' (quoted in Ingham, 2004, 134).

In a similar analysis, André Orléan has used the sociologist Émile Durkheim's concept of 'social representations' to 'grasp the reality of money, not as traditionally by the classic list of functions, but in its capacity to gain the general assent of the group as the legitimate expression of value' (Orléan,

2014b, 55). 'Social representations' of money endow it with power over us. Everyone must use it to value their own possessions and position in society and seek it – as the legitimate repository of value – as the means to acquire goods and more money. In contrast to the economic concept of value inherent in the utility of things in the 'real' economy, this sociological theory contends that *economic value* only assumes an *objective social existence* – that is, value recognized by all – in *money*. This resonates with Mirowski's claim that it is imperative for society to establish 'the working fiction of an invariant standard' (Mirowski, 1991, 579) and the necessity of Simmel's 'quasi-religious faith' for the stability of money (Simmel, 1978 [1907], 179). Money is *assignable* trust. In the face of real-world radical uncertainty, self-fulfilling long-term trust is rooted in a social and political legitimacy whereby potentially personally untrustworthy strangers feel able to participate in complex multilateral relationships. Historically, this has been the work of states.

In short, money ultimately depends on the viability of the social system in which it is created Again, Simmel grasped the link: 'The feeling of personal security that the possession of money gives is perhaps the most concentrated and pointed form and manifestation of confidence in the sociopolitical organization and order' (Simmel, 1978 [1907], 179). Disorderly societies have disorderly money and vice versa – causality runs from either direction. Monetary disorder and disintegration for the social scientist is akin to the engineer's experimental destruction tests. In severe crises, money's social foundations, normally masked by the hegemony of everyday life, are 'unveiled' (Orléan, 2008).

Money: Disorder and Disintegration

An important implication of a social theory of money counters the implication that departures from a well-functioning system are the result of flaws in money itself: that is, the wrong kind of money or the wrong kind of monetary policy. This is most obvious in the continued calls after bouts of inflation or debt crises that the precious metal standard is the only sound basis for money. Jean Cartelier refers to this as the 'hypostasis' of money: 'Money is not to be conceived of independently of the set of rules, implicit or explicit, which give sense to society where it is observed. Social phenomena in general and money in particular cease to be intelligible when they are severed from their context' (Cartelier, 2007, 227). Strictly speaking, money 'disorder' is a misnomer: when money ceases to perform as expected, we should look to the disorder of the 'implicit or explicit' rules of the social and political foundations of money.

Money's social nature is evident in its sensitivity to self-fulfilling fluctuations in its value. Inflation is accelerated by expectations of further price rises, which induce spending to pre-empt the anticipated loss of purchasing power. Similarly, foreign holders of currency, selling for fear that inflation might trigger a fall in the exchange rate, will cause further domestic inflation as the prices of imported goods rise. Consequently, central banks are primarily concerned with the management of expectations in their efforts to establish 'the working fiction of an invariant standard'.

There are three basic conditions in which money does not fulfil its functions: deflation, inflation, and, ultimately, disintegration, when the money of account for the denomination of value is abandoned.

Deflation

In certain circumstances, the 'fiction' of money as a *store of value* can perversely conflict with its other functions for the routine operation of the economy. In James Buchan's evocative term, money is 'frozen desire' which allows the temporary postponement of consumption and investment (Buchan, 1997). Holding money grants time to assess alternative courses of action, but clinging to 'frozen' value in response to insecurity and uncertainty induces a 'disorder' – as Keynes explained during capitalism's severe deflation in the 1930s. Holding on to money, described by Keynes as 'liquidity preference', produces a vicious circle. Reductions in spending and in finance for production and employment exacerbate the very same circumstances that created the uncertainty, insecurity, and pessimism. Furthermore, deflation encourages further postponement in the hope of even lower prices.

Consequently, central banks do not aim for zero inflation for fear that this might create expectations of falling prices and trigger deflation. There are many initial causes of depressions and deflation, but they often follow the frequently recurring debt-default crises in capitalism (see chapter 4). Building on Schumpeter's observation that capitalist enterprise is typically carried out with borrowed money, Hyman Minsky advanced his 'financial instability hypothesis' (Minsky, 1982, 36–7). Moderate cycles of 'boom and bust' are 'normal functioning events' in which the optimis'ic expansion of debt in search of greater profit increases balance sheet fragility and eventual defaults (see Ingham, 2011, 39–42 and Postscript). With the expansion of debt, default among weaker enterprises can rise significantly, causing a rapid widespread aversion to risk which stalls the expansion as loans are called in and banks reduce lending. The chain reaction of defaults in the sub-prime mortgage crisis that triggered the Great Financial Crisis in 2008 – known as the 'credit crunch' – was dubbed a 'Minsky moment' (Ingham, 2011, Postscript). We shall see that to avoid a repetition of the 1930s, governments acted with near zero interest rates and 'quantitative easing' to facilitate the availability of money that private banking and finance were unable and unwilling to supply (see chapters 4 and 7).

Arguably, however, deflation is more resistant than inflation to remedial monetary policy. Curtailing the demand for money or restricting its supply can often reduce inflation, but converse measures frequently fail to halt deflation. Merely pumping money into the economy has been likened to 'pushing on string': it does not necessarily stimulate consumption and production. Hence the Keynesian advocacy of fiscal policy. Governments should take responsibility to do what is not being done by the incapable unemployed and the unwilling capitalists and bankers: that is, create money and *spend* it. But for orthodox economics, this is precisely what is feared will eventually cause inflation when the supply of money runs ahead of the capacity of the 'real' economy to produce consumable commodities.

Inflation

A little inflation is not seen to be problematic; indeed, it is an indication that the economy is working at near full capacity in which high levels of demand create short-term shortages of supply, inducing price increases. Modern monetary policy attempts to achieve a low and steady rate of inflation of 2 per cent or so to avoid low and falling prices and a slide into deflation. None the less, central banks are constantly on guard against any hint that modest rates of inflation might surge (see chapter 4).

Very high levels of inflation are rightly feared by all members of society: for example, hyperinflation such as the daily doubling of prices in Zimbabwe in 2008 and Venezuela in 2019 creates chaos, leading to social and political disintegration. Hyperinflation – generally classed as a monthly inflation rate of 50 per cent and above – threatens the financial basis of the entire capitalist system. Banking grinds to a halt as the nominal rate of interest required to maintain a real rate of profit for lenders becomes unacceptably high for borrowers. Demand for loans falls and defaults rise. Unable to fulfil its functions, the currency may be abandoned in favour of alternative forms of money. With taxes unpaid and state finances in ruins, governments and states can collapse. In short, hyperinflation dissolves everything in its wake, throwing the entire fabric of society into anomic disarray: that is, social life loses all sense of meaning and order.

Strictly speaking, as money is inessential in the model of the 'real' economy, there can be no inflation; the demand and consequently supply of media of exchange are governed entirely by the availability of goods to be purchased. In mathematical Walrasian 'general equilibrium models', fluctuations in the value of money are eradicated by assigning a constant value to one of the commodities as the *numeraire*. Aside from this pure theory, more pragmatically oriented macroeconomics is concerned with the reality of inflation and aims to provide analyses which can be used by central banks to establish confidence that they can deliver monetary stability. Monetary policy will be examined in chapters 4 and 5; here, we will focus on more general theoretical issues in the explanation of inflation.

We have seen that the 'commodity-exchange' theory of money is closely related to 'quantity' theory, in which the price level is determined by the ratio of two quantities – of commodity money and of commodities. (We will ignore the problems of calculating the *general* price level as opposed to prices of specific commodities.) As we noted in the previous chapter, it has been widely assumed that Fisher's 1911 equation MV = PT represents a causal link, as expressed in the simplistic conception of inflation as 'too much money chasing too few goods'. In Fisher's time, inflation was not a problem; the value of money had remained stable for over half a century – in the late nineteenth century, prices of haircuts and shaving were etched in hairdressers' mirrors! The main concerns were, first, with the consequences of any increase in the supply of money that might follow gold discoveries and an influx of bullion; and, second, to warn against the creation of unsound inconvertible, 'intrinsically valueless' paper money such as the *assignats* in the French Revolution and the 'greenbacks' of the American Civil War (see Ingham, 2004, 19–22). Later in the twentieth century, these two experiments and the experience in Weimar Germany in the 1920s (see below) were invoked as proof of the dangers of government spending. Keynes's arch adversary Friedrich Hayek was quick to point to the threat of inflation posed by the state monopoly of currency supply freed from the gold standard constraint, which led him to advocate the denationalization of money and a system of freely created competing currencies.

Until well into the twentieth century, the almost exclusive focus on government spending led orthodox economics to overlook two distinctive elements of capitalist economies that could also cause inflation. Guided by the logic of commodity theory and the assumption that the gold standard was the acme of efficiency, 'quantity' theorists held to a firm distinction between 'money' – metal-based currency – and bank 'credit'. Consequently, they did not see that the 'credit' extended by bank lending created 'deposits' which became 'money' when spent in the wider economy by the borrower. This process could lead to a situation in which the assumed causality in Fisher's equation was reversed: that is, from

Prices to Quantity. Raised prices could be met by money created by debt – bank loans. Bank 'credit' was not money and therefore was excluded from the quantity of money in the equation. This possibility would have been clear if – in a further move away from 'classical' theory – the monopoly power of capital and labour to raise prices in 'imperfectly' competitive markets had also been acknowledged. In other words, the imposition of price rises met by the creation of money by bank loans is an inherent feature of the routine operation of capitalism.

With this more realistic view of the capitalist economy, some Keynesian analyses moved away from the direct focus on the money supply and looked at the growing inflation of the 1960s and 1970s in a way which is consistent with this reversal of the 'quantity equation'. Modest 'cost-push' and 'demand-pull' forms of inflation are typical of an economy operating at full capacity and employment. In 'cost-push' inflation, prices are 'pushed up' by increases in the costs of any of the factors of production – labour, capital, materials – when enterprises are running at full productive capacity. That is to say, with higher production costs and already maximized productivity, profits cannot be maintained at the same level of production. Consequently, in the absence of highly competitive markets, increased costs can be passed on to consumers by monopoly producers, contributing to a rise in the general price level. Keynesian models of cost-push inflation in which monopoly capital and labour have the power to raise prices are consistent with Marxist and sociological conflict models of inflation in which competing claims drive up wages (Rowthorn, 1977; Aquanno and Brennan, 2016; Hung and Thompson, 2016; Volscho, 2017).

On the other hand, 'demand-pull' inflation is closer to the more mainstream analysis of long-run capacity constraints on the economy. In an expanding economy, operating at full capacity, demands from households, businesses, governments, and foreign buyers compete for the finite supply of goods and services, bidding up prices and causing inflation. These mismatches between demand and supply are attributable to a wide range of factors. Demand could be increased, for example, by government purchases, tax cuts, and a currency depreciation inducing foreigners to spend more.

Keynes's observation that *expectations* about money – as opposed to the forces of the 'real' economy – could affect prices was eventually acknowledged by orthodoxy and ironically integrated into the fundamental tenet of the long-run neutrality of money in an ultimate equilibrium of supply and demand. Using Nobel Laureate Robert Lucas's 'rational expectations' theory, Thomas Sargent and Neil Wallace claimed to have refuted Keynesian economics by demonstrating that government expenditure to stimulate employment would be 'policy ineffective' (Sargent and Wallace, 1975). Based on the 'rational expectation' that monetary expansion creates inflation, economic agents would press for higher *nominal* wages, returning *real* wages, output, and employment to the previous level. This is not the place to examine critiques of 'rational expectations' other than to note that the history of inflation suggests that not all economic agents share the same 'rational expectations' as the economists who advanced the hypothesis! (For an accessible account of 'rational expectations', see Mankiw and Taylor, 2017, chap. 9; for a critique, Skidelsky, 2018, 194–7.)

However, there is no simple linear relationship between quantities of money and prices: for example, inflation remained subdued long after the loosening of monetary policy in the USA and UK in the 1990s; and, as we have noted, deflation is often unresponsive to monetary stimuli. The vast sums of money injected into the economy by the Japanese government and central bank have not jolted it out of the chronic deflation that has persisted since the financial crisis in 1990. This inconsistent correlation has become a central issue in mainstream economics' unresolved debate on the short run and long run. Regardless of the quantity of money, all manner of short-run phenomena – 'money illusion', false 'expectations', 'imperfect' information, and 'event shocks' such as exchange rate depreciation – can affect prices, but it is maintained that ultimately they will be determined by the ratio of the quantitative supplies of goods and money. Rising prices, indicating scarcity, either will stimulate an increased level of supply or, if it cannot be produced, will stifle demand, bringing inflation to halt in a new equilibrium.

A Social Theory of Monetary (Dis)Order

Disorderly – that is, unwanted and unanticipated – fluctuations in the value of money are an ever-present possibility. First, there are problems of knowledge and uncertainty. Apart from the limiting cases of extreme contraction and expansion – for example, how the dearth of money exacerbated the 1930s depression and how increasing the supply of money to meet rising prices is utterly self-defeating – we cannot know with any reasonable precision the effect of a given quantity of money on economic activity. Problems of defining, measuring, and controlling the supply of money led to the swift abandonment of 'monetarism' in the late twentieth century (see chapter 4), Based on probabilistic economic models, central banks' forecasts try to resolve the problems; but these are notoriously inaccurate the further the calculations are projected into the unknowable future. They are beset by Donald Rumsfeld's 'unknown unknowns'. Consequently, monetary authorities can only hope that their efforts will sustain self-fulfilling expectations of the stability of money.

Second, the structure of the monetary system and the quantity that it supplies are the result of conflicting interests. Money is never merely a neutral instrument adopted by *homo economicus* in pursuit of 'utility', nor a 'public good' provided by a disinterested monetary authority. The power to create money – monetary sovereignty – has been vigorously contested throughout history, and consequently monetary disorder is almost inevitable. There are three broad money interests. The first are issuers who claim the right to declare what counts as money – that is, the means for settling debt – and to regulate its supply. We have noted Aristotle's indictment of money's destabilization of politics in Classical Greece; Oresme's challenge to the French king; and the government and Currency School resistance to the Banking School's advocacy of decentralized money; and in chapter 7 we will examine the latest conflict over the production of money in the wake of the Great Financial Crisis. Two other interests reside at opposed sides of the credit–debt relations which are an inherent consequence of the use of money. On the one hand, creditors and holders of money wealth press for strict control over the supply of money to safeguard the value of their assets and loans against devaluation due to inflation. Historically, they have favoured 'hard' money in the form of a fixed metallic standard, strict controls on government spending, and high interest rates. On the other hand, producers and consumers are more likely to be debtors, for whom a 'soft' or a loose control of money meets their demands and, if inflationary, reduces the real value of their debt. And, of course, sovereign money creation – from medieval monarchs to modern governments – gives the power to avoid or escape indebtedness. Creditors – medieval landowners and buyers of government bonds – insist that state expenditure is funded by revenue and not by the inflationary manipulation of money. We have noted the efforts of medieval monarchs and we will see that bondholders are the major constraint on modern governments (chapter 4). In short, levels of supply and demand for money are not determined exclusively by actual or predicted productive capacity and the availability of commodities in the 'real' economy. Rather, money is a contested source of economic, social, and political power, and the impact of the struggles on how and how much money is created is always uncertain.

Third, conflict over the distribution of economic returns in society is obviously expressed in monetary claims. Myriad equally endowed individuals in economics' perfect competition model can only be 'price-takers': that is, single individuals do not have the market power to affect prices. But powerful interests in real-world capitalism are 'price-makers' who are able to make a monetary claim to a greater share of the social product. In chapter 4, we shall see how economic distributional conflict in the 1970s had an impact on economic theory, policy, and monetary institutions. In Latin American populist democracies in the twentieth century, 'printing' money to buy support and placate conflicting claims proved to be counterproductive. The inflation and instability that followed simply exacerbated discontent.

It follows that a truce in the 'struggle for economic existence', leaving the existing distribution of wealth and income uncontested, is a necessary condition for price stability. Peaceful economic co-existence may express a balance of power in society in which no interest is able successfully to impose its demands; or there may be contentment with the existing normative equation of worth and reward in which a 'fair day's' work' receives a 'fair day's' pay'. Any such social equilibrium or consensus is invariably closely related to a state's effectiveness in maintaining social order, and consequently to its legitimacy. Confidence in a state and its money are inextricably, but precariously, intertwined. An effective and legitimate state may successfully moderate or supress the 'struggle for economic existence'. In the UK immediately after 1945, a certain type of monetary policy was underpinned by a social consensus, or 'settlement' between economic interests – both of which disintegrated in the 1970s (see chapter 4).

There are also many possible *external* sources of monetary instability: for example, inflation triggered by a narrowly economic event such as a falling exchange rate and a consequent rise in the price of imports might lead to discontent and a loss of government legitimacy. The converse is equally possible: a weak government might shake foreign holders' confidence in the currency, resulting in a sell-off and a falling exchange rate, followed by rising inflation as the prices of imported goods increase. And, of course, the collapse of a state by defeat in war or internal revolution almost invariably entails the destabilization of its money. The complexity of the relationships between causes and consequences of monetary disorder preclude any simple conclusions. But it cannot be emphasized too strongly that monetary stability is never merely an economic question; political and social instability leads to monetary instability and frequently monetary collapse. The following account of hyperinflation is presented as an extreme – almost 'experimental' – illustration of the interrelated totality of social, economic, and political factors involved in money disorder.

Disintegration: Weimar Germany's Hyperinflation, 1921–3

The nature of money and its social and political bases were starkly 'unveiled' first by the disintegration of the German state and its money in hyperinflationary chaos after 1921 and then by its sudden end in 1923 (Orléan, 2008).

Following military defeat in 1918, revolution swiftly transformed Germany from a stable monarchy into the fragile Weimar democratic republic, governed by a succession of weak coalition governments comprising squabbling socialist, progressive, and centre parties (see Feldman, 1996; Evans, 2002). The order of the pre-war authoritarian state gave way to unprincipled scrambling for gains by striking workers, rebellious soldiers and sailors, rapacious landlords, profiteering industrialists, and their fragmented political representatives. Socialists consolidated their place in the new democracy with full employment policies, an eight-hour day, increased pensions, unemployment insurance, and welfare. A rapid renewal of production was encouraged with tax breaks and aid for industrial corporations. Escalating demands were made and hasty concessions granted against the backdrop of a demoralized nation and a bankrupted state facing vast war reparations from the victors. The crisis of the German state was soon manifest in a crisis of a core component of a state's sovereignty: its money.

From the outset, confidence in both state and currency was low. Restoring the pre-war mark with the promise of its gold convertibility was out of the question; the country was devoid of gold reserves. Without this constraint on the issue of currency, competing domestic demands and reparations payments were met by simply printing money. The 'gold mark' was retained as the nominal money of account against which the value of the paper currency was established at a notional, but unrealistic, 1:1 ratio. By 1923, the ratio had become 1:1,000,000,000 (one thousand million or one trillion). Notes with a face value of 100 million marks failed to slow the increasing volume of paper money. Distribution of notes by vast train-loads and in the later stages by aeroplanes could scarcely keep up with the insatiable demand to meet the dizzying rise in prices, described at the time as the 'delirium of the milliards' (Fergusson, 2010 [1975], 39).

Rudolph Haverstein, President of the Reichsbank, apologized for not being able to produce and deliver notes quickly enough to keep pace with the rise in prices. Proponents of the quantity theory of money alleged that he was misguided by the German 'state theory' of money into thinking that the increased quantity of money had not, in the first instance, caused the rising prices. And, in a sense, Haverstein was right; he was justified in claiming that rising prices were caused by the two intractable problems facing Germany: paying for the reparations imposed by France and Britain and acceding to the demands of the militant factions to avoid a further revolution. Creating money was the only immediately available solution; Haverstein and the government decided that stopping the production of money at this stage would cause utter political and social disintegration.

Furthermore, the 'hard' currency (dollars, sterling, or gold) for reparations payments could only be bought with newly printed rapidly depreciating paper marks. This pushed the exchange rate from 8 marks to the US dollar in 1919 to 320 in 1922, at which point the reparations had to be paid in coal: that is, 'surrogate' money (see chapter 6). Near the end of the hyperinflation in 1923, the dollar–mark exchange rate was a meaningless 1:4,000,000,000,000,000. Depreciation of the mark exacerbated the domestic price inflation, caused by the printing of money to meet the leapfrogging claims for wages and pensions, and by big business's profiteering.

Once in motion, the hyperinflation was self-generating. Rising prices were met by ever-increasing claims for higher wages and greater profits, which in turn were met by faster production of more money, which was spent on receipt in a near futile attempt to avoid further inexorable depreciation. Many contemporary accounts gave vivid testimony of the social disorientation. A French observer concluded that continual rapid changes in the value of money made it impossible to establish from day to day even the approximate wealth of anyone or anything (Orléan, 2008, 31).

The government had neither the will nor strength to stop the printing. Moreover, during the first year of hyperinflation in 1921, the two main protagonists in the anarchy had no wish to call a halt. Both the organized working class and their profiteering employers in the large monopolies were able to keep abreast or even ahead of inflation (Ahamed, 2009, 123). Borrowing to expand production was accompanied by an immediate and rapid depreciation of the debt. Squeezed between the two powerful interests, middle-class functionaries, teachers, public employees on fixed incomes, and non-unionized workers were impoverished to the point of starvation. By 1922, a clerk's yearly salary was barely enough to keep his family for a month (Fergusson, 2010 [1975], 84).

People eventually began to balk at pushing wheelbarrow-loads of notes to buy bread. (It is a telling indication of monetary calculation's fundamental importance for daily life that people held onto the incalculable money of account for as long as possible.) Eventually, the mark was abandoned after it became utterly unusable for pricing and purchasing goods. Farmers' refusal to accept money for their produce was an important turning point. City dwellers raided the countryside, crudely slaughtering livestock and stealing food – social and political order had disintegrated.

The end of the hyperinflation in October 1923 was so sudden as to be a seen as a 'miracle'. Monetary stabilization by the issue of a new paper currency (Rentenmark) by a new bank (Rentenbank) perfectly illustrates money's social and political foundations and the relative unimportance of economic factors in establishing its acceptability. A political coalition of the capitalist and landed property owners of the Rentenbank promised that new Rentenmarks would be backed by legally contracted mortgages on German property. This was purely fictitious; the validity of the claim was dependent on that which was yet to be established: that is, the value of the mortgages depended on the successful stabilization of the Rentenmark (Orléan, 2008).

In short, monetary stabilization had to await a political agreement between the main interests embroiled in the chaotic struggle in which the emission of money was both cause and consequence of their enmity. The political settlement encouraged a suspension of disbelief; the *Rentenbank* was able to replace the worthless paper notes with the new ones simply because they were not the old ones (Fergusson, 2010 [1975], 216). New prices were quoted in new marks simply by cutting twelve zeros from extant old mark prices, which 'miraculously' now remained stable.

We will now re-engage with the development of the distinctive element of modern capitalism: the elastic creation of credit money as *capital*.

PART II

CAPITALISM AND MONEY

4
The Evolution of Capitalist Money

Means of payment in a state money of account is the most prevalent money in modern capitalist societies, but state monetary sovereignty is not absolute. First, money creation is shared with privately owned banks. One of capitalism's distinctive characteristics is, in effect, a franchised and regulated banking system which produces money 'endogenously', denominated in the state's money of account – transmitted by cheques and debit and credit cards – in addition to 'exogenous' money issued by central bank cash and emitted by government spending. This shared creation of money places limits on central bank control of the money supply and is the source of a further academic and political controversy (see chapter 7). Second, capitalist contract law permits the creation of private acknowledgements of debt (promises to pay, IOUs, etc.) which circulate as means of payment in financial networks. This 'near' money overlaps with and penetrates the franchised banking system, further diluting control of the supply of money and, in certain circumstances, competing with state money. This 'near' money is part of a monetary hierarchy in which forms of money are ranked by the ease of their conversion into state money: that is, their 'liquidity' (Bell, 2001; Ricks, 2016). Non-state forms of money will be examined later, but we begin with a sketch of the evolution of the institutions which produce the state and bank money which sits at the top of the hierarchy in modern capitalism.

This development may be divided into two broad periods. The first, between the sixteenth and early twentieth centuries, saw the fusion of states' precious metal currency with merchants' private credit with which they conducted their business. In the second phase, starting in the early twentieth century, money's link to precious metal gradually came to an end. When money could no longer be identified as a naturally scarce valuable substance, it became more difficult to disguise its true nature as a 'social technology' with the potential to be created to advance collective welfare.

The 'Template' for Modern Money: the Fusion of Public and Private

Between the sixteenth and nineteenth centuries in western Europe, three separate institutions became linked in the 'template' for the creation of forms of money that are now almost universal. First, states produced currency – based on a money of account of a real or 'imaginary' precious coin – which, in turn, was accepted as payment of taxes. Second, private banking networks issued and managed the exchange of bills in mercantile trade, accepted deposits, and extended loans to rulers and governments. Third, states granted a charter to a privileged private bank to manage their debt by raising loans from private merchant capitalists. Eventually, the state-chartered banks became the 'central' banks which controlled and regulated the private banking network, stabilizing crises by acting as 'lender of last resort' (Ingham, 2004; Calomiris and Haber, 2014; Vogl, 2017).

The core element of this process was the gradual integration of the private banks' notes and bills with the public currency issued by states in payment for goods and services. As with all money, the private notes were issued as a 'liability': that is to say, issuers promised to redeem their own notes as payment for any debt that they were owed. For example, 'free banking' in the USA, between 1837 and 1886, allowed the issue of notes by banks and almost any organization: railroad companies, churches, restaurants, and so on. In England, the 1844 Bank Charter Act granted exclusive note issue to the Bank of England and prohibited any new bank from issuing its own notes. Mergers and concentration in banking during the nineteenth century effectively created 'new' banks which gradually reduced the number of note issuers – the last in Britain, Fox, Fowler and Company, closed in 1921.

Today, legal tender money is created by both the state and the banking system. States issue payment for goods and services, usually by drawing on their account at their central bank. And the regulated banking system has a state-granted franchise to issue the legal tender, denominated in the state's money of account, by extending loans to borrowers. That is, capitalism contains a social mechanism by which these private debtor–creditor contracts are routinely 'monetized'. The links between the state, central banks, and the banking system transform *private debt* into *public money*.

As we explained in chapter 1, modern banks lend by creating a deposit of *new money* for the borrower with taps on the computer keyboard. (This differs from the coinage era, where loans reduced the money-lender's hoard.) The pervasive influence of the commodity theory of money is evident in the commonplace description of this process in economics textbooks as the creation of money 'out of thin air' – or *ex nihilo*. However, 'thin air' is not involved; rather, modern bank money is *socially* created by the borrower's legally enforceable *promise* to repay the debt. The deposit is a *private debt* owed to the bank which becomes *public money* when it is spent by the borrower. At this juncture, its origin as a private debt is utterly irrelevant to whoever receives it as payment. This modern 'alchemy' achieves what the medieval efforts to turn lead into gold failed to do.

Bank customers' deposits are owed by the bank to the depositors and consequently are the bank's *liabilities*. The existence of deposits created by the bank as loans (the borrower's *debt/liability*) is based on the promise of repayment and consequently they are classed as the bank's *assets*. If necessary, the bank's assets and liabilities can be balanced by borrowing from other banks in the network and from the reserves that it is required to hold at the central bank.

The issue of money – or, more accurately, its *emission* in payments made by the state – similarly involves debts and credits which are managed by the state treasury and central bank. Payment for state expenditure is made by the treasury from the state's account at the central bank. Unless a state and its central bank have adopted a precious metal standard and convertibility of paper notes, the money is emitted by 'fiat': that is, declaration. (Consequently, as we saw in chapter 2, Modern Monetary Theory contends that the sovereign monetary power can spend money into existence and, in practice, does not require the prior collection of taxes.)

The inflationary potential of an unlimited emission of fiat money is constrained by the rules and norms of 'sound money': that is, to make it 'scarce' by specifying a prudent balance of expenditure and revenue. Government deficits, created by an excess of spending over tax revenue, are financed by borrowing with the sale of interest-bearing bonds to private finance capital in the money markets. Here judgement is passed on the acceptability of a government's fiscal position: that is, the balance between revenue and expenditure. This assessment is based on conventional wisdom in the financial community and the monetary authority, which is in turn influenced by mainstream academic economics. If it is thought that government expenditure risks inflation by putting 'too much' money into the economy, money markets might demand higher interest rates to offset the risk. It is important to note that there is no single unequivocal answer to the question of 'how much' money, created by government spending, is 'too much'. Any judgement depends on many factors, including the most favoured of the many different answers to the question given by the competing economic models that are the stuff of academic dispute.

This production of modern capitalist money will be examined in more detail in the following chapter; here we outline how this was the result of conflict and cooperation between the state and private mercantile money in a public–private partnership. The European 'commercial revolution' of the fourteenth and fifteenth centuries created a wealthy merchant class which in Max Weber's phrase formed a 'memorable alliance' with the state, laying the foundations for modern capitalism.

Weber's analysis of the western origins of capitalism has been criticized for its 'Eurocentric' view of modern history, which neglects commerce and banking in East Asia. However, the relationships between state and capital in East Asia differed from the alliance forged in Europe (Ingham, 2015). In broad terms, there are three types of merchant capital–state relationship. First, there is *isomorphism*, in which the state is also a merchant trading company, as in the Italian city-state republics. For example, the merchant republic of Venice was in effect a joint-stock trading company with the Doge as its president, the Senate its board of directors, and the populace its shareholders. Second, there is *mutual exclusion and unresolved antagonism*, as in China. For example, Chinese banking was inhibited by the fear that deposits might be plundered by local and central government. And, third, there is *mutual accommodation and interdependence*, as in the 'memorable alliance' of the monarchy and/or government and merchants in Holland and England. (Ingham, 2004, chap. 7; Calomoris and Haber, 2014, chap. 4). It is to this type of relationship that we turn now.

The 'Memorable Alliance'

By the fifteenth century, parts of western Europe – in particular, a corridor from Italy through Burgundy to Holland – were sufficiently pacified to support the expansion of long-distance trade. Networks of merchants used private credit money (promissory notes, bills of exchange) that were netted out and settled at regular intervals at 'fairs' – notably, in Champagne and Besançon. (The denomination of the credits and debts in the merchant bankers' own unit of account also enabled them to make profits by arbitraging fluctuating exchange rates between state moneys of account and their own [Boyer-Xambeu et al., 1994; Ingham, 2004].) The merchants' money conflicted with the efforts of the monarchs to establish monopoly control of their currency and territory. Minting coins was both a symbol and a real source of sovereignty, consolidating fiscal power and creating opportunities to profit from seigniorage and the manipulation of the money of account, as noted in chapter 2. The existence of mercantile money also diluted sovereign revenue by tax avoidance, as still occurs today.

During the fifteenth and sixteenth centuries, these two paths of monetary development eventually merged to create the distinctive capitalist monetary system (for a full discussion, see Ingham, 2004, chap. 6; Vogl, 2017, chaps 2–4). The first step was taken in the Mediterranean city-states, where – unlike the northern monarchies – the form of government favoured the integration of private mercantile money and state money. 'Public' banks were established by the governing merchant class in these bourgeois city-state republics: Barcelona (1401), Genoa (1407), and, most importantly, Venice's Banco della Piazza di Rialto (1587). They were established to convert merchants' loans to the city government into transferable bonds, based on the state's promise of repayment. Consequently, they were widely accepted as a means of payment in addition to the coined currency. In effect, the rulers of the bourgeois republics were borrowing from and lending to each other and using their IOUs as money. Marx believed that the state had been 'alienated' to the bourgeoisie.

However, the superimposition of private and public debt in the city-states was a source of instability. Acceptability of the state's bonds could be impaired by merchants' defaults and political conflict in the governing mercantile plutocracy. None the less, a new 'social technology' for creating money had been developed which was to achieve more stability in northern Europe, where it was based on an interdependence – as opposed to superimposition – of bourgeoisie and state.

During the sixteenth century, some northern European monarchies gained greater control of their sovereign monetary spaces, prohibiting the circulation of foreign coins, restricting the use of bills of exchange, and strengthening their metallic money. Elizabeth I's comprehensive recoinage in England during 1560–1, establishing four ounces of silver as the standard for the pound sterling, greatly enhanced confidence in the currency. Ironically, however, a strong metallic currency led to a scarcity of money and many monarchs became increasingly dependent on loans from merchants to finance their wars. Defaults were common, intensifying the conflict between sovereign and bourgeoisie. As early as 1339, for example, Edward II of England defaulted on a Florentine debt which was worth the annual Florentine production of cloth at the time (Arrighi, 1994, 103).

Charles II's default on his debt to the London merchants in the 'Stop on the Exchequer' (1672) was the catalyst that led to one of the most significant events in the development of modern capitalist money. Discontent among ruined merchants increased bourgeois support for 'Dutch finance', which had been established in Amsterdam in 1609. Modelled on the techniques developed in the Mediterranean city-state 'public banks' for the creation of credit money, Amsterdam's Wisselbank converted loans into transferable bonds and notes.

Following Charles II's death in 1685 and the accession of James II, the London merchants and parliamentarians invited the Dutch Prince of Orange to invade and accede to the English throne as William III in the 'Glorious Revolution' of 1688. The offer of the English throne came with strings attached. 'Dutch' public banking was established, but William had to accept a constitutional and fiscal settlement involving financial dependency on parliament and the bourgeoisie. London merchants provided £1.2 million of capital for the foundation of the Bank of England in 1694 to arrange long-term borrowing to finance William's expenditure – mainly on the wars to weaken competitors' trade. The £1.2 million of capital, loaned to the king and his government at 8 per cent interest, was to be funded by taxes and duties. In the new financial technology, the king and his government's *promise* to service the debt to the Bank of England became its *asset*, on which it was able to issue its own banknotes to private borrowers for the same amount of £1.2 million, *doubling the creation of money*.

In effect, the 1688 constitutional settlement in which sovereignty was now located in the 'crown-in-parliament' had subtly transformed the king's *personal* debt into the *'national'* debt. (As described in chapter 1, this is the same as the modern bank creation of deposits in the form of *public* money for a borrower, based on his or her promise to repay the *private* debt to the bank.) This 'national' debt became a perpetual and permanent loan which is never repaid, binding creditors to the state by their receipt of continuous annual interest. The ownership and control of the public – or 'national' – debt by numerically very small capitalist interests remains a definitive element of modern states, making them literally 'capitalist states' (Hager, 2016).

Marx grasped this incisively:

> As with the stroke of an enchanter's wand, [the public debt] endows barren money with the power of breeding and thus turns it into capital, without the necessity of its exposing itself to the troubles and risks inseparable from its employment in industry or even in usury. The state creditors actually give nothing away, for the sum lent is transformed into public bonds, easily negotiable, which go on functioning in their hands just as so much hard cash would. (Marx, 1981 [1887]: 529)

Modern capitalism's creation of money was grounded in the fiscal norms that the 'memorable alliance' had laid down, linking the state, creditors, and taxpayers in antagonistic interdependence. The state now depended on both financiers and taxpayers; continuous loans required dependable taxation to service interest payments on the debt. During the eighteenth century, efficient bureaucratic tax collection became one of England's 'sinews of power' (Brewer, 1989). However, taxes were unpopular; creditors were wary of a state default or the inflationary erosion of the investment by excessive state spending; and states had to mediate between these demands whilst pursuing their own interests.

Over the course of the eighteenth century, hundreds of local 'country' banks were established, using the same process for producing new money. Deposits created by borrowers' private debts to the bank became the assets for the issue of banknotes which existed alongside the minting of coined currency, augmenting the money supply. Backed by the sovereign and government's promise to pay interest on the debt, the Bank of England's notes were in most demand, enabling it to profit by accepting local notes at a discount in exchange for its own. Consequently, Bank of England notes began to circulate widely in the monetary space defined by the pound sterling money of account that Elizabeth I had stabilized at 4 ounces of silver.

Despite the apparent opposition between the two forms of money, expressed at the time by the age-old dispute on the nature of money between William Lowndes and John Locke, the banknotes and metallic currency were complementary. Gradually, it was realized that an exclusively metallic coinage restricted state expenditure and economic expansion; but without the precious metal standard, confidence in banknotes, as 'claims' on currency money, would have been weaker. In 1692, Sir William Petty, Oxford Professor of Anatomy, and founder member of the Royal Society, posed a rhetorical question: 'What remedy is there if we have too little money?' To which he replied: 'We must erect a Bank, which well computed, doth almost double the effect of our coined currency' (Hull, 1997 [1899], 446).

The integration of the two forms of money in England – private bank credit and state currency – was made possible by a resolution of the conflict between the bourgeoisie and the monarchy. The constitutional settlement reordered the antagonistic relationship between crown *and* parliament as 'crown-*in*-parliament'. The *modus vivendi* was the result of the delicate balance between too much state power, which might have suppressed mercantile banking, and too little state power, which might be insufficient to sustain a linchpin metallic currency to underpin the bank money.

The history of the USA illustrates how the forging of a monetary system, based on the integration of state and banking money and mediated by a central bank, can be inhibited by unresolved economic and political conflict. Fearing that bankers' power posed a threat to agrarian interests and the government's control of money, President Thomas Jefferson opposed Alexander Hamilton's 1791 charter for the Bank of the United States. Eventually, the charter was granted and renewed in 1816, but regionally based economic and political conflict persisted. After a further renewal was refused, the Second Bank of the United States was liquidated in 1841 (Calomiris and Haber, 2014).

The USA was without a central bank until the founding of the Federal Reserve in 1913 in response to the serious banking crisis six years earlier. The central bank's federal structure was an attempt to satisfy conflicting economic and political interests by giving twelve regions their own reserve banks. But this simply incorporated the conflicts into the banking system – especially, the Midwest's opposition to New York's Wall Street connections. 'Crippled by populism', a decentralized, fragmented, and unstable banking system persisted well into the twentieth century (Calomiris and Haber, 2014, 153).

Regional, economic, and political conflict in the UK was never great enough to stall the gradual extension of the Bank of England's control and management of the monetary system. During the late nineteenth century, it finally assumed the role of 'lender of last resort' in financial crises triggered by bank defaults and panic cash withdrawals from other banks. Lending to viable banks to save the system from collapse had been advocated since the 1840s, but Walter Bagehot's *Lombard Street* takes the credit for its acceptance. To halt a stampede for cash, he argued that the Bank of England should restore confidence by lending 'most freely . . . to merchants, to minor bankers, to "this and that man", whenever the security is good' (Bagehot, 1873, 51). The Bank of England's intervention provided the rationale for establishing the US Federal Reserve and almost all other central banks (Calomiris and Haber, 2014).

By the late nineteenth century, Britain's combination of a 'sound' gold-based currency and a robust banking system, founded on the world's leading economy, had become the monetary model to be emulated. However, at the pinnacle of its success, the gold standard's inherent weaknesses were exposed.

'The Barbarous Relic'

During the early twentieth century, it became clear that it would be increasingly difficult to fulfil the promise to redeem bills and notes in gold. Indeed, the metallic standard could only continue if notes circulated without being presented for conversion. This was even more obvious at the international level, where trade payments were made with the bills and notes of credit issued by London's merchant banks (de Cecco, 1974). Quite simply, the quantity of available gold was unable to maintain a credibly stable relationship with the volume of payments required by the vast expansion of global capitalism.

Furthermore, demands for greater state expenditure, especially to deal with the economic dislocation and depressions in the aftermath of the First World War, could not be met if governments maintained the gold standard constraint on the money supply – the 'golden fetters' (Eichengreen, 1995). In

Keynes's view, the 'the barbarous relic' should be abandoned (Keynes, 1971 [1923], 172). (Ironically, the USA's belated adoption of the gold standard in 1900 occurred almost precisely at the time that it became increasingly difficult to maintain.)

A glimpse of the reality of modern money that lay behind the golden façade was revealed at the outbreak of the First World War in 1914, which was followed by large-scale selling of stocks and runs on banks, paralysing continental financial systems. Panic spread to London and queues formed outside the Bank of England demanding the exchange of convertible banknotes for gold sovereigns. Fearing the rapid exhaustion of the meagre gold reserves, the government closed the banks by declaring a four-day Bank Holiday. The Bank of England suspended gold convertibility; raised interest rates to 10 per cent to attract deposits; transmitted a massive infusion of credit to the banking system; and bought the London banks' outstanding credits that could not be settled by continental banks.

The most novel measure was the issue of £300 million of ten shilling (10/-) and one pound (£1) notes by the Treasury – not the Bank of England, which had only £9 million of gold. Signed by the Secretary of the Treasury John Bradbury, the 'Bradburys' were calmly accepted by the public and the crisis was averted. This was the first significant direct issue of money by the state. Although grateful for their salvation, the bankers balked at this circumvention of their profitable business in interest-bearing government debt. They insisted that the Treasury should not issue any further 'interest-free' money; if not backed by gold, money must be based on established practice, in which the state's promise to repay debt was the Bank of England's asset on which further notes could be issued. Furthermore, government debt incurred by the war must be financed in the time-honoured way with money borrowed at 3.5 per cent annual interest from the private sector, rescued in 1914 with public money. (See chapter 7 for the comparable rescue after the Great Financial Crisis in 2008; and also the question of 'interest-free', 'sovereign' money.)

The episode had shown that it was possible to create viable money without either gold or the arrangements between private finance capital and state debt that had evolved since the late seventeenth century. But, at the time, none of the parties had any wish to abandon the 'memorable alliance' and its linkages between the state, its central bank, and the banking system. Rather, the ruling elite in the institutional nexus between City finance, state Treasury, and the Bank of England attempted to recreate the pre-war world and Britain's former power (Ingham, 1984). The domestic and international gold standard was controversially reintroduced in 1926, but ignominiously abandoned following a European banking crisis in 1931. Now, if the supply of money were no longer fixed to a naturally scarce precious material, could it be a resource at society's disposal to improve human welfare? With the extension of the franchise in western democracies and the onset of the Great Depression in the 1930s, the question took on more urgency.

Modern Money: War and Democracy

With Britain's inability to maintain the gold standard, international monetary arrangements entered a period of instability in which no major economy was willing or able to manage its currency as a 'world money' for international trade. As the strongest currency, the US dollar was best placed to take on the role, but the government was unwilling. The reluctance probably reflected the fact that the fragile US banking system and its inexperienced, devolved, and politically fractious Federal Reserve were incapable of managing the dollar as international money. The absence of an adequate quantity of globally acceptable means of payment exacerbated the stagnation of world trade and the economic slowdown, which led to protectionism, nationalist populism, and, ultimately, the Second World War.

The collapse of the gold standard constraint on the supply of money was not immediately followed by the abandonment of the conventional fiscal orthodoxy of balanced budgets and 'sound money', which remained underwritten by economic orthodoxy. None the less, worldwide crises during the 1930s Great Depression brought some relaxation of monetary policy, especially in the later New Deal programmes in the USA. However, the apparent success of massive spending on public works by the Communist and Fascist regimes was met with scepticism. It was conceded that these measures might create employment in the short term, but the 'Treasury view' prevailed in Britain. Based on the 'classical' economic tenets of 'neutral' money and the 'real' economy, it held that levels of public spending in excess of revenue would ultimately lead to inflation.

The struggle for control of money in the capitalist democracies now began in earnest. Keynes and others gave a theoretical basis to the efficacy of money, arguing that 'effective demand' created by government spending induced virtuous circle of production, employment, and consumption. But these ideas were not generally accepted until during and after the Second World War, which wrought two important changes, influencing the way money was created and controlled in Britain and the USA. First, techniques were developed for the management of the entire economy as if it were a single enterprise. With Keynesian theory, the government control of materials, labour costs, and, above all, money laid the foundation for more proactive economic strategies, as opposed to piecemeal reaction to crises. Second, the Second World War tipped the balance of political and economic power in the democracies in support of government spending to ensure well-being and employment. Mass participation of populations, as both combatants and targets of bombing, had given further impetus towards social democratic policies that had been hesitantly pursued during the first half of the twentieth century. Now, governments were under pressure to fulfil their promises of recompense for the privations that populations had endured. The struggle for control of money creation entered a new phase.

The Post-1945 Domestic and International Monetary Order

As the war came to end, the Allies began to plan the reconstruction of the world economic and political order. It was essential that pre-war economic nationalism and protectionism was replaced by a liberal international economic system, which, in turn, required an internationally accepted means of payment. The question was addressed at Bretton Woods, New Hampshire, at a conference of British and US officials in 1944. Leading the British delegation, Keynes submitted a proposal for a new stateless world money which he whimsically dubbed the 'bancor' (*banc* [bank], *or* [gold]): that is, paper money underwritten by the participating nations. Keynes's proposal would have diffused power among the participants, but, wishing to avoid dilution of its post-war dominance, the Americans rejected it. Instead, they insisted that the dollar, valued at $35 per ounce of gold, was to be the linchpin global currency against which the exchange rates of all others were to be established by collaboration between national central banks and the newly established World Bank and International Monetary Fund.

Adopting a gold-dollar standard gave considerable power and advantages to US governments and Wall Street's international banks. As the fixed linchpin, the dollar could not be affected by the currency market's assessments of the strength of the US economy and the size of government debt. Consequently, the USA was free to decide on interest rates and a money supply to suit its needs; and US corporations and banks gained profits and a competitive advantage from the dollar's status as world money. In the words of the French Minister of Finance, Valéry Giscard d'Estaing, in 1965, it was 'an exorbitant privilege' (Eichengreen, 2010; see also Gowan, 1999). In the same way that the pound sterling enhanced British hegemony during the gold standard era, the dollar after 1945 was the USA's most potent weapon in the international 'struggle for economic existence'.

Although it was agreed that international free trade was the best means of achieving growth, Keynes had argued that these principles should not be applied to money. Speculation on international money and capital markets could impede the domestic economic policy commitments to full employment and social welfare. As Keynes explained:

> There will continually be a number of people constantly taking fright because they think that the degree of leftism in one country looks for the time being to be greater than somewhere else. . . . [T]he whole management of the domestic economy depends on being free to have the appropriate rate of interest without reference to rates

prevailing elsewhere in the world. Capital control is a corollary of this. (Keynes, 1978, 149)

The pursuit of full employment and social welfare required that governments were able to control two monetary factors: interest rates and the currency's exchange rate. Interest rates affected the level of investment and employment; and exchange rates had an impact on the price of imported raw materials and of exports and, consequently, on employment. Control of international capital movements was to prevent speculative trading of currencies, based on variations and differences between countries in interest rates and inflation prospects. Controls restricted the purchase of foreign currency to its use as a medium of exchange and payment in international trade – Keynes's money "a mere intermediary' (Keynes, 1971 [1923], 124). For a while, the states retained the control of money that they had taken from the banks during the war, revising the balance of power with private money-capital in their favour. But we shall see that this proved impossible to maintain when the resumption of economic growth inevitably resuscitated the power of global capitalist banks and corporations.

A New 'Alliance' and the Long Post-War Economic Boom

From the late 1940s to the early 1970s, the USA, western Europe, and some East Asian countries experienced unusually high and sustained growth, together with full employment and low inflation – capitalism's 'Golden Age'. During this period – with some variations – there existed a broad social democratic political consensus in western capitalism based on an application of Keynesian economics. Government deficit spending in advance of revenue could increase the levels of 'aggregate demand', leading to employment and, consequently, increased tax revenue to balance the government's accounts. Moreover, full employment and welfare provision were linked in further positive feedback: employed workers would need less welfare, which their taxes would help to finance.

'Free market' economic orthodoxy was moved off centre-stage, but its advocates continued to insist that government control of the economy and monetary system to pander to the electorate was not only economically irresponsible but also the political 'road to serfdom' (Hayek, 1994 [1944]). Deficit government expenditure did not express the 'real' capacity of the free market economy to produce output and employment and would ultimately create a supply of money in excess of the economy's needs, resulting in inflation.

The acceptance of deficit finance was an expression of a readjustment of the powers involved in the creation of money. Enhanced government control led to measures which became known as 'financial repression' (Reinhart and Belen Sbrancia. 2011). Governments aimed to reduce the cost of servicing the interest on their massive post-war debt and much-needed new loans by maintaining very low or even negative real interest rates. This was done by manipulating the financial system to reduce returns on financial investment to lower levels than would be expected in a free market. Caps were placed on interest rates on government debt and bank deposit rates. A captive domestic market for government debt was created by requiring banks to increase their capital requirements by holding government bonds. The export of finance in search of higher returns overseas was curtailed by capital controls introduced as part of the post-war Bretton Woods international monetary system. As Keynes envisaged, the pursuit of full employment required the integrated and coordinated control of both domestic and international money.

This shift in the balance of power in capitalism was also evident in the disadvantage to the financial sector of the economy and those classes which managed and lived on accumulated and invested wealth: the 'rentiers'. Taking the Bank of England into public ownership in 1946 gave governments the power to enact 'financial repression'. They could now control the banking system more directly in order to keep pressure on interest rates, reducing the cost of borrowing needed to cover deficit spending. However, this 'repression' of the state's creditors was a renegotiation not a repudiation of the terms of the time-honoured 'memorable alliance'. The state did not directly create money as it had done briefly with the issue of 'Bradburys' in 1914.

From 1945 to the late 1960s, there was an economic, social, and political equilibrium, or 'settlement', in many western democracies which was based on the way in which money was created and managed. Capitalist enterprise, organized labour, and financial classes (rentiers) accepted a revised distribution of rewards. Capitalism's 'Golden Age' of high levels of employment, steady rates of growth, and low inflation resulted in real increases in wages and profits, producing relative contentment after decades of depression and war. In the absence of alternatives, the disgruntled rentiers had little choice but to accept the revised terms of their deal with the state. Of course, there were political and economic crises; but these were never serious enough to doubt that the turmoil of the 1930s had been eliminated. As ever, governing elite hubris was eventually dashed by capitalism's volatility and its ever-shifting balance of power. Satisfaction with the new status quo among classes and economic interests was short-lived and there was a renewed struggle to control the creation of money.

The Disintegration of the 'Golden Age'

By the late 1960s, a range of factors converged to bring an end to the domestic and international political settlements and agreements upon which the economic and monetary management of the 'Golden Age' depended. During the early 1970s, moderate levels of inflation in many western economies began to accelerate to over 10 per cent, reaching 26 per cent in the UK by 1976. Opponents of Keynesian economics seized on this as evidence for their theoretical critique of government deficit spending, but although there was a revival of orthodox monetary theory, matters were not so straightforward. As the suddenness of the inflationary surge was not closely correlated with an increased money supply, it was clear that other forces were involved. External factors such as the OPEC oil price rise and exchange rate instability played a part. However, a major driving force of inflation was generated by the very conditions that had initially sustained the post-war social and political equilibrium: full employment and rising real wages.

The wage–price spiral and inflation crises of the 1970s were expressions of a shift in the balance of power and associated changes in social and cultural expectations (Smithin, 1996; Ingham, 2004, 153–9; 2011, 81–8; Hung and Thompson, 2016). Full employment had removed the restraining influence of Marx's 'reserve army' of the unemployed and had empowered and emboldened organized labour forces. Commenting on wartime promises to maintain full employment, the Polish economist Michał Kalecki had presciently argued that governments would eventually have deliberately to deflate the economy to dampen the workers' new-found power and expectations of ever-increasing wages (Kalecki, 1943). By the middle of the 1960s, 'relative satisfaction' with peacetime full employment of the 1950s had given way to 'relative deprivation'. Rather than satisfaction in gratitude for respite from the past privations of their class, workers compared themselves with other classes and expected even better times.

The democratizing influence of the Second World War and the resumption of mass consumption capitalism, exhorting the working classes to participate in the 'affluent' society, were powerful solvents of Britain's traditional social order. With purchase by instalments and the removal of restrictions on bank loans, a place could be secured in a new status order based on 'conspicuous consumption'. As noted in chapter 3, increased levels of oligopoly enabled firms to accede to wage demands and simply pass on the increased costs in higher prices for consumers. A wage–price spiral was set in motion: firms and their workers both raised their prices, which were financed by money produced by loans from the banking system.

Inflation not only nullified nominal wage increases and provoked further demands, but also eroded real returns on financial investments to the point where they became unacceptably negative. The rentier and creditor classes grew disaffected with the post-war 'repressed' low rates of interest, which they had been prepared to accept if their returns were not completely erased by inflation. As Kalecki had forecast, interest rates were raised to constrain the money supply, deter borrowing, and placate creditors by restoring positive real returns on investments. However, there is a limit to how far interest rates can rise before a wave of defaults on loans and a fall in borrowing for investment and consumption stall the economy. Moreover, it was politically and economically necessary to resume economic growth and full employment without incurring inflation. To achieve this, governments eventually turned to the old economic orthodoxy, which had never been entirely displaced by Keynesian economics. However, we shall see that the real 'war on inflation' was not only waged with ideas but also fought in a battle for the control of money, which involved the removal of trade unions' power successfully to claim higher wages.

The 1970s domestic inflationary crises were closely associated with the breakdown of the other political agreement that was designed to underpin the post-war Keynesian governance of capitalist economies in the West: the Bretton Woods international monetary system. As world growth gathered pace after the war, it became increasingly difficult to control capital movements and foreign exchange transactions. Checking and matching trade invoices to authorize the release of foreign currency for payments was cumbersome; and the recovery and expansion of transnational corporations and banks simultaneously greatly increased and hampered the monitoring of capital flows. However, the greatest source of these flows and the most serious threat to Bretton Woods was the very thing upon which it was based: the dollar. More precisely, it was the vast reservoir of dollars that the US balance of payments deficits had flooded into the world that proved to be decisive. These expatriate dollars fed the formation of unofficial parallel money and capital markets alongside the Bretton Woods system – most notably, the euro-dollar markets based in London that emerged in the late 1960s (Helleiner, 1994; Burn, 2006).

Efforts to counter these developments were ineffective; but the final blow came in 1971 when the USA decided that its interests were no longer served by maintaining the Bretton Woods system of a fixed relation between the dollar and gold. After years of erosion, this brought an end to the regulatory regime of capital controls and managed semi-fixed exchange rates which had allowed a greater degree of domestic control of economic policies. If anything, the USA's 'privilege' was now even more 'exorbitant'. It retained all the advantages of having the dollar as *de facto* world money without the responsibility of managing the Bretton Woods system (Gowan, 1999). With the lifting of restrictions, the USA was able to attract foreign capital to finance growing deficits incurred by the Vietnam war and domestic 'Great Society' expenditure. Wall Street was opened to global capital on 'May Day' 1975, setting in motion a process of 'competitive deregulation' in which the leading states opened their markets to fund their borrowing and to give their banks access to profits from dealing in capital flows. By 1995, 61 per cent of all central bank reserves, 77 per cent of all bank loans, and 48 per cent of trade invoices and prices – including all-important oil – were in dollars (Gowan, 1999).

There had been a dramatic tilt in the balance of power from states to private capital in the creation and management of money. Buying and selling on global currency markets – for both international trade and speculation – once again determined exchange rates. The advantage to states of access to foreign capital to finance their debt came at the cost of a loss of control over exchange rates and interest rates. Consequently, as Keynes had envisaged, domestic and social policies were constrained. In these changed circumstances, any government's attempt to manage its exchange rate or interest rates to achieve policy goals faced the insoluble 'tri-lemma' of simultaneously achieving all three of the following: (i) fixed/stable exchange rates for currencies; (ii) domestic autonomy in control of interest rates by central banks; and (iii) unrestricted foreign exchange markets – that is, free international capital mobility. With floating exchange rates, it was only possible to exert some control over either interest rates or exchange rates, but not both.

For example, a currency's rising exchange rate, caused by speculation, could affect employment by raising the price of exports. However, countering this by lowering interest rates to reduce foreign demand for a currency might lead to more domestic borrowing, increasing the money supply and possibly inflation. And, of course, any hint of inflation would be likely to deter foreign investment in government bonds. Conversely, a falling exchange rate increased the cost of imported raw materials; but an increase in interest rates to halt the exchange rate fall might depress domestic investment and consumption, raising unemployment.

Revising the Terms of the 'Memorable Alliance'

At the end of the 1970s, after a decade of political and economic conflict and crises in western democracies, the struggle for the control of money took a decisive turn – most notably in the USA and UK. The primary objective of 'Thatcherism' and 'Reaganomics' was to expunge inflation and restore positive real rates of return on invested capital. In this 'revenge of the rentiers' (Smithin, 1996; Volscho, 2017), the ideological and political significance of academic theories of money was never more apparent. During the late 1970s and early 1980s, the neoliberal and 'monetarist' critiques of Keynesian macroeconomic policy were established (Pixley, 2018; Skidelsky, 2018; Smithin, 2018).

In his revamping of the 'quantity theory' of money as 'monetarism', Nobel Prize winner Milton Friedman reasserted the nineteenth-century axiom that 'inflation is always and everywhere a monetary phenomenon in the sense that it is and can be produced only by a more rapid increase in the quantity of money than in output' (Friedman, 1970, 24). The main source of any increase was held to be government spending in excess of the capacity of the economy to produce the goods to soak it up. An elaboration identified the mechanism by which government spending generated inflation. Government payments created 'exogenous money': that is, 'outside' the market economy. When deposited by the payees into the banking system, it became 'high-powered' money by increasing the size of the 'fractional reserve' on which the banks could make loans 'multiply'. Holding a 10 per cent 'fractional reserve', for example, a bank could lend £90 for every £100 deposited, which, in turn, would 'multiply' further when deposited in another bank(s): that is, £90 minus £9 'fractional reserve' equals £81 million of lending capacity, and so on. 'Monetarist' theory held that reductions in government spending would prevent this 'multiplication' of money from exceeding the private sector's capacity to produce 'real' output. Furthermore, pragmatic monetarists believed that an insistence that there was a finite quantity of available money might act like the gold standard and initiate a 'self-fulfilling prophecy' that prices could not rise.

Embracing 'monetarism', the USA and UK introduced money supply targets which would be met by the reduction of government spending's emission of money into the economy. The first targets were for 'narrow money': that is, cash (M0) and easily converted bank deposits such as chequing accounts (M1). Less liquid, but increasingly important, forms of money – such as savings time deposits, credit cards, and 'near money'– were classified as 'broad money' (M2, M3, and M4) and initially not targeted. Furthermore, the rapid growth of 'broad money' was ironically accelerated by the Thatcher government's deregulation of the UK's financial system, which removed time-limits on some deposits, increasing their liquidity: that is, their convertibility into cash. The deregulation's unintended expansion of the money supply fuelled an inflationary 'boom' of rapidly rising house prices in 1989, followed, as ever, by a 'bust'. By 2006, the originally most illiquid category (M4) had increased to £1,250 billion from £25 billion in 1984 (Lipsey and Chrystal, 2011). (By 2010, the total money supply was measured at £2.2 trillion, while actual notes and coins in circulation were only £47 billion – a mere 2.1 per cent of the total.)

After consistent overshooting in the UK, the targets were revised upwards and abandoned entirely in 1984. The failure of 'monetarism' was largely a result of its faulty foundations: the greater volume of money is created not 'exogenously' but 'endogenously' by loans in the franchised banking system. This lending does not depend on the prior existence of a level of 'fractional' reserves provided by deposits, including those of governments' 'high-powered' money to its payees. As we noted earlier in this chapter, in the 'alchemy' of capitalist banking, loans make deposits and reserves can be sought later.

Governments fell back on controlling the demand for money by raising interest rates, which had an impact on inflation but at the expense of employment. In the UK, inflation fell from 18 per cent in 1980 to around 5 per cent in the middle of the decade; but unemployment doubled from 1.5 million to over 3 million during the same period. Unwittingly echoing Kalecki's prediction forty years earlier, some politicians saw unemployment as a temporary strategy for reducing labour's power to make successful wage demands. Money had undoubtedly become a 'weapon' in the struggle for economic existence. In a reversal of post-war Keynesian macroeconomic policy, taming inflation had replaced employment as the government's main economic policy.

However, the power of trade unions to claim a larger share of the national income had to be permanently curbed. Consequently, between 1980 and 1993, the UK's Conservative governments introduced legislation to restrict unions' ability to back claims for higher wages with strikes. Deliberate confrontation in the UK during the 1980s – most notably the coal miners' strike in 1984–5 – resulted in defeat for the labour unions, a loss of power, and a decline of membership. However, changes in the balance of power in the economy were not entirely attributable to legislation and confrontation. By the late 1970s, heavy industries such as mining and iron and steel production, which were the basis for the strong labour unions, were in decline in the established western economies. These and other changes in the structure and conditions of employment, including a return to casual labour, seriously weakened the trade unions. The removal of organized labour's power, together with global competition, has resulted in stagnant real wage growth and an absence of inflation in the western economies so far during the twenty-first century.

Global Capital, Independent Central Banks, and Monetary Policy

By the 1980s, the main activity on foreign exchange markets was no longer the acquisition of means of payment for international trade – Keynes's 'mere intermediary'. Speculation on currency values accounted for 90 per cent of transactions, exacerbating exchange rate volatility. Currencies were traded rapidly in response to any indication that government debt might be 'unsustainable': that is, inflationary or leading to default. Conversely, 'safe' currencies were bought in the expectation that their value would increase. As Keynes and others had envisaged, futile attempts to defend exchange rates and/or interest rates had an impact on the pursuit of domestic economic policy. The balance of power in the control of money had shifted further from states and governments to markets. In the attempt to bring some stability and predictability to the markets' judgement of the prospective value of their currency, governments were compelled to establish a credible commitment to controlling inflation. They did so by formally abnegating the control of their money, handing it over to their 'independent' central bank.

A constant theme in money's history has been the attempt by the leading monetary power to remove money from the arena of social and political conflict. 'Metallism' assigned it to the natural realm, but with the end of the gold standard and the rise of representative democracy, this was no longer possible. In many capitalist economies during the last quarter of the twentieth century, the depoliticization of money took the form of granting formal independence to central banks (for an account of the relationship between central banks and democracy, see Pixley, 2018; Tucker, 2018). The control and management of money was handed to technocratic experts, informed by economic theory, in institutionally independent central banks. 'Independence' is interpreted differently in both principle and practice, but the general aim was to detach monetary policy from manipulation by governments bent on pandering to the electorate with inflationary expenditure. 'Independence' can be seen in terms of Carl Schmitt's understanding of sovereignty as the power to decide the 'exception': that is, the decision to act outside established law and convention (Schmitt, 2005, 5). 'Independence' organizes money as 'the decisive exception in capitalist liberal democracy. . . . [T]he monetary realm is posited as the domain of absolute, non-democratic sovereign authority in modern capitalist states, and . . . this virtually unaccountable power is justified by the claim that without it, liberal democracy would fall apart' (Mann, 2013, 199). A comprehensive account of central banks since independence by a former senior Bank of England official, Paul Tucker, concludes that alongside the judiciary and the military they have become the 'third great pillar of unelected power' (Tucker, 2018, ix). As we shall see in the following chapter, the European Central Bank (ECB) was granted 'exceptional' autonomy from the European democratic governments by the Maastricht Treaty (1992). This was more easily accomplished for the ECB because there was no unified European state to which it might be attached – the euro is a 'stateless' currency.

The evolution of capitalist money shows that control of its creation and the uses to which it is put cannot be understood simply as the result of the application of economic 'science'. The current system for creating money is also the result of conflict over what is to count as money and who produces it. Theories of money have played their part and, indeed, it could be said that the persistence of the unresolved 'incompatibility' between the two main theories is an expression of the ongoing struggle for command of money's power: neutral instrument or force of production?

5

Modern Money (i): States, Central Banks, and Their Banking System

We begin with a highly simplified description of how money at the top of the hierarchy is typically created in the major capitalist economies, building on the analysis of the development of the 'template' laid down by the alliance between sovereign states and private capital. However, there is one notable and very important exception to these typical arrangements: the eurozone. Here the monetary space circumscribed by the money of account and its currency is not co-extensive with a *single* sovereign state. We shall see that this has been a significant factor in Europe's recent monetary and political crises.

'Top' Sovereign Money

In all stable capitalist states, the money in most demand is produced by the links between the state treasury, the central bank, and the franchised banking system. 'Top' money is often referred to as 'legal tender': for example, 'this note is legal tender for all debts public and private' is printed on US Federal Reserve bills. In practice, however, the concept of 'legal tender' has become increasingly ambiguous: for example, the total value of contactless card payments has overtaken the state's cash in many modern economies – with the notable exception of Japan. The ambiguity is also evident in some economists' classification of private bank deposits

– transmitted as payment by cheques and cards – as 'inside' (market, or non-state, 'endogenous' money) as opposed to 'outside' (outside the market, 'exogenous') state money. However, deposits in banks regulated by the state's monetary authorities, denominated in the state's money of account and accepted as tax payment, are *de facto* franchised state money. Together with notes and coins, immediately accessible deposits and those with short-term maturity are classified as 'broad money' – the main component of total money supply – by the monetary authorities in most countries. Transmitted by electronic transfer, they are accepted as public money or 'legal tender' and are readily converted into currency: for example, as 'cash back' in supermarkets. None the less, in many states there is no legally enforceable obligation to accept these forms of bank-issued payment, but, with certain exceptions, cash payments cannot be rejected.

The following account focuses on the institutional architecture of these interrelations between the state treasury, the central bank, and the franchised banking system. However, it should be borne in mind that the acceptability of money produced in this way is always conditional. The coercive power of the state to make payments and to enforce taxation in its own money can never be enough for the routine operation of a monetary system. As we have emphasized, money also requires legitimacy and the suspension of disbelief in its all too apparent fragility. Successfully institutionalized money shifts the onus of trust in transactions from the *direct* and *personal* level to the *indirect* and *impersonal* trust in the issuers' ability to produce stable money. For most of money's history, this confidence was based on its 'naturalization' as an intrinsically valuable substance. Today, expert economist technocrats, assisted by the attribution of charismatic intuition to some central bankers such as Alan Greenspan at the Fed, are now the authors of the 'working fiction' of stable money (although Greenspan's 'charisma' diminished when he confessed to a US Senate committee in 2008 after the Great Financial Crisis to having held a 'flawed' theory of efficient markets). Ultimately, however, trust in the stability of money is dependent on the legitimacy and political stability of the state; failed states invariably have failed money.

Central Banks

The central bank is the centre of a network between itself, the state treasury, and the franchised banking system, coordinating the relationships between the public and private monetary and financial sectors. There are considerable variations in these relationships between different states (Calomiris and Haber, 2014; Pixley, 2018; Tucker, 2018), but three closely linked core functions of central banks can be identified: (i) acting as the state's banker; (ii) producing stable money; and (iii) acting as 'lender of last resort' to the banking system.

The State's Banker

Originating as privately owned banks with a charter to organize loans to governments, central banks occupy a structurally ambiguous position. Straddling the public and private domains has important consequences for how they operate. Most are now state-owned, but some – most notably, the US Federal Reserve – remain formally private institutions performing exclusively public functions which, as we shall see, have important consequences for private capitalism.

The sovereign power to issue and redeem the means of payment, by accepting it in settlement of debts owed to the state, is the linchpin of the entire economy and society. This power resides in the complementary links between the treasury and central bank, governed by the accountancy rules and norms of state finance that have evolved since the late seventeenth century. State treasuries make payment for government expenditure with funds drawn on their accounts at the central bank (see Wray, 2012, chap. 3; Pixley, 2018, 50–6). If tax and other revenue is insufficient, treasuries are permitted only under exceptional circumstances to 'monetize' their debt by borrowing *directly* from the central bank or to issue their own currency – such as the British Treasury's 'Bradbury'notes during the First World War. To repeat: the historical arrangement between state and finance capital requires that treasuries borrow by issuing bonds, through the central bank, to the money market for final purchase by banks, pension funds, insurance companies, and private individuals.

Strong states' bonds are the safest investments in modern capitalism, normally attracting willing buyers. However, if necessary, borrowing by the treasury for the funding of government expenditure can be almost guaranteed by the central bank's provision of the necessary money reserves to the banking system to make it possible to purchase the bonds. As the US Federal Reserve Chairman, Marriner Eccles, explained to Congress in 1947:

> The fact that [the Treasury] cannot go directly to the Federal Reserve bank to borrow does not mean that they cannot go indirectly to the Federal Reserve bank, for the very reason that there is no limit to the amount that the Federal Reserve can buy in the market. . . . [I]f the Treasury has to finance a heavy deficit, the Reserve System creates the condition in the money market to enable the borrowing to be done, so that, in effect, the Reserve System indirectly finances the Treasury through the money market. (Quoted in Tymoigne, 2016, 1329)

Direct 'monetization' of government debt is anathema, but *indirect* monetization is accepted practice – highlighting the ambiguity of capitalist states' public–private monetary systems.

The Pursuit of Stable Money

As we saw in the previous chapter, 'monetarism' failed fully to understand that the money supply was not primarily the result of its 'exogenous' transmission into the banking system by government spending. It was thought that this 'high-powered' money was the main constituent of the 'fractional reserve' which was the base for the 'money multiplier'. As we noted, however, money is largely created 'endogenously' by bank lending, which does not require the prior existence of reserves. Rather, banks lend and then seek reserves, provided by central banks at a 'base' or 'overnight' rate, to maintain solvency (see also Ryan-Collins et al. 2011; Tucker, 2018). In other words, money creation operates in the opposite direction to the one in the 'money multiplier' model (Goodhart,

2009). This recently received belated semi-official acknowledgement in the *Bank of England Quarterly Bulletin* in 2014, endorsing credit theory's contention that all money is an IOU that the issuer promises to redeem by accepting it as payment in settlement of any debt. That is, money's value is given by the value of the debt that it can settle.

Consequently, the *Bank of England Quarterly Bulletin* also agreed that in 'normal times' inflation can only be controlled by interest rates to influence the demand for money. But, of course, the level of control is compromised and limited by the shared sovereignty in the dual private–public system. In 'normal times', most central banks cannot authoritatively impose interest rates on the banks; rather, they use their ultimate money-creating power to manoeuvre banks into conforming. The rate set for lending to the banks in the franchised system is intended to be the 'benchmark' which will influence all other borrowing rates. In 'normal times', this rate cannot be mandatory; rather, it is a 'target' that the central bank aims to hit by using its own greater power to create money. As noted, banks borrow from the central bank at its 'base', or 'overnight', rate to balance their books in the short term, which it is hoped will be the platform on top of which the private banks set the interest rate on loans to customers. In turn, this will strongly influence demand for money-creating loans and the total supply of money. For example, the Bank of England's Monetary Policy Committee decides on an appropriate 'benchmark', or 'base', rate which it is thought will balance price stability and economic growth: high rates to deter borrowing and check possible inflation and low rates to encourage borrowing for production and consumption.

However, banks are not compelled to borrow if they have their own ample reserves or can find funds at a more attractive rate elsewhere. If so, the central bank will not achieve its target rate and desired impact on the money supply. We shall see in the following chapter that central bank control of the money supply can also be weakened by the availability of privately issued IOUs ('near money') in the 'secondary', or 'shadow', banking system. Therefore, the central bank influences the franchised banks' need to borrow at its 'base'/'overnight' rate by using its money-creating power to manipulate the level of the banks' reserves. In conjunction with the treasury, the central bank buys and sells government bonds on the money market ('open market operations'). Bond purchases put money in the banking system and bond sales remove it from the banks' reserves – consequently, influencing their capacity to create money by lending. By attempting to calibrate the supply of money in this way, the central bank tries to exercise a degree of control over the demand for its reserves and, consequently, the 'target' interest rate and, in turn, the demand for money.

Again, in this private–public partnership, the banking and financial system's purchase of government debt is not based on direct compulsion by the central bank. Clearly, the central bank has the ultimate power of lending in 'last resort' to safeguard the system. But bank and government bond investors' compliance is also grounded in so-called 'moral suasion' and confidence in the assurance that the level of government spending will not lead to an inflationary erosion of the value of their safe investment. During the 1970s inflation in the UK, there were 'gilt strikes': that is, there was a refusal to buy government debt unless deflationary policies were introduced (on the power struggles between central banks, the banking system, and investors in the money markets, see Pixley, 2018).

With the further globalization and deregulation of financial markets during the 1980s, 'bond vigilantes' in international financial markets and credit-rating agencies became the major force in judging what are prudent levels of government spending. Establishing the credibility of the currency's inflation credentials to reassure the money and financial markets is now one of the central bank's primary goals. If bond markets lack confidence in government policies, they will require a higher rate of interest to attract demand, which will consequently increase the cost of borrowing – as the governments, for example, of Portugal, Greece, Argentina, and countless developing countries know only too well.

In pursuit of these goals, as we saw in the previous chapter, many central banks were granted formal 'independence' from government control to lend credibility to 'sound money' credentials and reassure increasingly powerful foreign exchange and money markets. Most central banks aim to keep inflation below a target, usually between 2 and 4 per cent, using a 'benchmark' interest rate to influence demand for money. The desired non-inflationary supply of money is calculated using the most generally accepted 'new macroeconomic consensus' models (see Pixley, 2018, chap. 7; Skidelsky, 2018, chap. 4). Here money is a 'neutral' instrument for coordinating the 'real' economy comprising variables – employment, rates of interest, inflation, and so on – which are deemed to have a 'natural' level, objectively determined by their contribution to the economy's equilibrium. For example, the models are used to determine the 'non-accelerating inflation rate of unemployment' (NAIRU): that is, the level of employment which is consistent with a steady low rate of inflation (see Skidelsky, 2018, chap. 4). In short, it is claimed that the question of the appropriate supply of money can be determined objectively by economic science and therefore should be removed from the political arena.

Globally prestigious universities play an important role in establishing the hegemony of a shared consensus based on academic economics. In this way, decision-makers in central banks, the International Monetary Fund, organizations such as the OECD, credit-rating agencies, and the global money and financial markets come to form an 'epistemic community' by which the central banks' actions and the markets' reactions are rendered intelligible and 'reasonable'. To achieve this, deliberations are formally recorded and communicated following a consistent procedure: that is, decision-making should be 'transparent'.

This framework strongly implies that there can be no rationally objective basis for opposed interests in the economy. In this view, there exists a theoretically optimum supply of money which maintains the equilibrium, which, by definition, is beneficial to all sectors of the whole economy. Dissent from the independent bank's measures can only come from the disruptive illegitimate pursuit of sectional interests based on mistaken theories which will bring sub-optimal solutions to the universally desired goals of efficiency and equilibrium. To some extent, effective control of money in non-authoritarian regimes requires that the population shares – or, at least, doesn't question – this hegemonic ideology. This enables monetary authorities and governments to resist creating money to appease demands when it is no longer possible to hide behind the pretence of 'intrinsically' scarce and valuable gold.

'Lender of Last Resort': Rescuing Capitalism and Finance-Capitalists

The threat posed by banking crises brings the pivotal importance of money into even sharper focus. Aside from the disruption of investment for production and employment, the day-to-day fabric of the capitalist economy's payments and contracts is immediately placed in jeopardy. In 2008, central bankers and governments were terrified; saving the financial and banking system was deemed to be essential to prevent utter disintegration.

Banking systems are linked by complex networks of debt which render all banks – regardless of the health of their balance sheet – vulnerable to some extent to the failure of any of the participants. In the late nineteenth century, as we noted in the previous chapter, Bagehot recommended that the Bank of England should lend 'most freely' during a crisis. Saving banks with sound balance sheets, who were in danger through no fault of their own, would halt a potential chain-reaction of debt-default, preventing wholescale disintegration, and, at the same time, reward the prudent. Gradually, the Bank of England took on this role. Reluctance in the USA to establish a central bank, noted earlier, was finally overcome by the need to deal with serious crises in the early twentieth century.

In the immediate aftermath of the Great Financial Crisis (GFC), the Federal Reserve went much further than 'lending in last resort' to endangered but solvent banks by also acting as '*dealer* of last resort' (Mehrling, 2011). The Fed took on the outstanding unsaleable assets of the entire money and securities markets. This not only ensured the continuity of the market for government bonds but simultaneously also rescued all private firms in virtually the whole range of financial markets. Central banks perform a public function by lending to halt crises but, given the structure of the monetary and financial system, this necessarily entails saving privately owned capitalist banks. In this case, the Fed went much further by granting much of US finance-capital immunity from the discipline of the market. This ensured the continuous operation of the market in government securities which is essential for government finances and, of course, its creditors' stake in the capitalist state. This rescue focused attention on central banks' ambiguous location between the private and public financial sectors – especially the legitimacy and autonomy of their actions in relation to democratic government. Was the rescue of private capital with the money of taxpaying citizens democratically accountable and legitimate (Pixley, 2018; Tucker 2018)? We will return to these questions in chapter 7.

Although banking systems had been saved in 2008, it was feared that capitalism might yet be thrown into a more serious depression than the 1930s. In earlier academic life, Ben Bernanke, Chairman of the Federal Reserve, had concluded that the 1930s Depression had been prolonged by persistent high interest rates and by allowing the money supply to remain restricted. Bernanke and other central bankers moved to avoid a repetition of the 1930s by cutting their 'base' interest rates to near zero, followed by 'quantitative easing' (QE) of the money supply. The measures brought the routine mechanism for creating money, involving government treasuries and central banks, to wider public scrutiny.

Cutting 'base' interest rates to near zero to encourage borrowing for investment and consumption was also equally important in reducing the cost of borrowing for highly indebted governments. However, maintaining low rates required that they were prevented from rising in response to any increased demand by the banking system in the market for monetary reserves. To supply the money to pre-empt this occurrence, central banks again tapped on their keyboard to trigger QE.

Contrary to widely held opinion, the only unusual feature of the operation was its magnitude – the means for creating the money followed established procedure. Although this was erroneously reported in the media as 'printing money', QE was conventional *indirect* money-creation involving the reciprocal manoeuvres between the three main agencies – (government) treasury, central bank, and banking system – and their assets. The treasury issued and sold government bonds, via the central bank, to the banking and financial system which were subsequently repurchased by the central bank with money it had created electronically by the tapping of its keyboard. Central bank payments for the securities were added to the banks' reserves, eliminating the possibility that any increased demand for money by the banks would cause interest rates to rise. Since the GFC, the US Federal Reserve has purchased almost $4 trillion of bonds and the Bank of England over £3.5 billion. By 2017, the leading six central banks that had used QE – the Bank of England, the Federal Reserve, the Bank of Japan, the European Central Bank, the Swiss National Bank, and Sweden's Riksbank – held 20 per cent of public debt (*Financial Times*, 16 August 2017). With access to this new money and the ability to borrow at the now very low interest rate from the central bank, the banks had no need to raise interest rates to attract deposits.

QE funding followed the procedure in which government (*public*) debt must *appear* to be financed by private capital – even if the *private* capital is provided indirectly by the state's (*public*) banker. Although not intended in the original agreement between king and merchant bourgeoisie, establishing sovereign debt, managed by the Bank of England, became the means to check the arbitrary sovereign power to create money, or manipulate its value, to finance expenditure (see chapter 4). In the past, this could be done by debasement or an alteration of the money of account (see chapter 2). Following abandonment of the 'gold standard' constraint on the creation of money, the temptation to 'print' fiat money to fund expenditure is checked by the bond market's reaction. If it is judged that government expenditure is potentially inflationary or that interest payments might lead to an 'unsustainable' burden for governments, the markets will be reluctant either to finance any deficit by purchasing government bonds or to demand a higher return. States with a capitalist economy are truly 'capitalist states' in the sense that they are largely funded by private capital (Hager, 2016).

In chapter 7, we will examine the responses to the questions raised by QE. Was it a necessary or indeed a legitimate use of the 'public purse'? Are simpler, more accountable democratic methods available? Is private capital's power to exert a strong influence on the terms at which it is prepared to lend a *necessary* check on profligate government expenditure? In the eurozone, the GFC shone a stark light on these and other questions.

The Anomalous Euro

With minor variations, the relationships between states, treasuries, and central banks, which produce a nation's sovereign money, are typical of all major capitalist countries, with one significant exception: those in the European Monetary Union, or eurozone. Here, there are two departures from the norm: first, the *fiscal* and *monetary* domains have been separated; and, second, the central bank is not a part of a sovereign power. The pre-1914 Austro-Hungarian Empire is the only other case in which the independent constituent countries shared a common currency but retained their national budgets (Goodhart, 2003 [1998], 195, n. 1).

Member states of the eurozone control their taxation and government spending and the European Central Bank (ECB) is responsible for the euro, which was introduced as a money of account in 1999 and as a means of payment in notes, coins, and electronic transmission in 2002. In the absence of a single sovereign state of Europe to which it would be attached, the ECB is the most 'independent' of all the independent central banks; the 'exception' of its power and autonomy is unmatched and unprecedented. The historic link between monetary sovereignty and state sovereignty has been broken, which many see as the basis for the eurozone's enduring monetary and economic problems (Bell and Nell, 2003; Ingham, 2004; Wray, 2012; Varoufakis, 2017).

For some orthodox economic theory, the single European currency is a logical counterpart to the single European market. If 'real' values, embodied in the costs of the factors of production, are uniform within a region, then it is an 'optimum currency area' (OCA). For example, an area is 'optimum' for a single currency if labour is sufficiently mobile within it to allow supply and demand to bring about uniform wage rates (see the discussions in Bell and Nell, 2003). Europe was obviously not an OCA at the time the Common Market was created in the late 1950s: costs of production varied considerably owing especially to the impact of different systems of welfare and social insurance on labour costs. None the less, OCA theory was a template. Given free movement of labour across the European Union (EU), the theory could be used to justify enacting measures to harmonize labour law, welfare expenditure, and other conditions which might eradicate these differences and create the 'real' economic foundation for a common currency.

Of course, the European project was also driven by geopolitical and other non-economic motives, but OCA theory was understood to offer objective economic grounds for monetary unification. Confidence in the viability of the stateless euro is based on the belief that the market, as it is understood in economic theory, is – or should be – the ultimate foundation for social order. The theoretical rationale for the EU's inter-state federalism and the economic Common Market is based on the Hayekian belief that economic transactions bind societies together in webs of advantageous interdependence. In this conception, money is not – as Simmel insisted – a bond with society (see chapter 3), but is merely the 'neutral' measure and representation of economic links. The 'state' and 'credit' theories of money provide a better understanding of the euro's short but troubled history (Goodhart, 2003 [1998]; and Ingham, 2004, as developed by Otero-Iglesias, 2015).

Following the logic of the theory of the 'real' economy and 'neutral' money, it was thought that the creation of a single currency, managed by a stateless central bank, would permanently pre-empt profligate government spending and inflation. An academic member of the ECB Board, Otmar Issing, could not have expressed economic orthodoxy more succinctly: 'the euro represents depoliticised and hence stable money' (quoted in Otero-Iglesias, 2015, 355). Similarly, the first European ECB President, Wim Duisenberg, explained that 'the euro, probably more than any other currency, represents the mutual confidence at the heart of our community. It is the first currency that has not only severed its link to gold, but also its link to the nation state. It is not backed by the durability of the metal or by the authority of the state' (quoted in Otero-Iglesias, 2015, 354). (If so, one might ask precisely how it is backed; or, following the 'neutral' money orthodoxy, Duisenberg might have been implying that money really didn't require to be backed.)

The surrender of monetary sovereignty by the member states was reinforced by their agreement to abide by common stringent fiscal rules and limits, which was intended to placate the global bond markets and suppress domestic demand for government spending. The rules and conventions in capitalist states that prohibit treasuries from borrowing directly from the central bank ('monetization' of debt) were given strict interpretation in the formal terms of the Maastricht Treaty (1992) and the Growth and Stability Pact (1997). These treaties laid down the fiscal and monetary foundations for the euro and the role of the ECB. Member states' fiscal control was severely restricted by the prohibition of budget deficits greater than 3 per cent of GDP and a debt-to-GDP ratio of above 60 per cent.

With a stateless central bank divorced from independent states' government finances, the 'memorable alliance' between state and capital had been significantly modified. As we saw in Chairman Eccles's explanation of the US Fed's role, discretionary central bank accommodation of government spending and capitalist funding had developed as the linchpin of sovereign state finances. The detachment of the ECB from the member states prevented this accommodation of their funding requirements; but we shall see that the GFC of 2008 created pressure to conform to the arrangements that had evolved in single sovereign states over the previous centuries.

Strict conformity to Maastricht fiscal rules left little room for discretionary budgeting and deficit spending by member states. Unlike counterparts outside the EU, they were required to establish their fiscal position in relation to revenue (taxation) and borrowing in advance of any expenditure – in the same way as any private enterprise raising finance from the money, bond, and stock markets. Raising taxes before spending was politically unpopular, and to attract loans from the global money market, member states were drawn into competitive fiscal stringency, enhancing the power of global finance-capital. Eventually, some of the more powerful governments – notably the French – were able to flout the fiscal rules.

However, from the early days of the European Economic Community, some European politicians were aware that –

notwithstanding the economic theory of OCA – a single currency was not viable without a single sovereign polity with its own independent fiscal policy, as argued by the 'state theory of money' and shown by history (Bell and Nell, 2003; Goodhart, 2003 [1998]; Ingham, 2004, 188–96; Otero-Iglesias, 2015). Indeed, the suspicion that the single currency was an almost inevitable step along the path to a single European state was one of the reasons for the UK's decision not to adopt the euro. Events since have added weight to these views. It is now more widely believed that the separation of fiscal and monetary sovereignty has played a large part in the euro's difficulties, which can only be resolved by their reintegration.

The single currency and fiscal–monetary separation pre-empted the deployment of separate policy measures to deal with individual cases of economic inequality and structural differences among member states. Economically uncompetitive members of the eurozone have been deprived of the right to adjust their current account deficits by currency devaluation to stimulate exports and restrict imports. Rather, these weak economies – Portugal, Italy, Greece, and Spain – have had to adjust by 'internal devaluation': that is, a reduction of nominal prices by cutting production costs, especially wages and social welfare. In neoliberal circles, this was welcomed as the application of market discipline to remedy economic inefficiency. The resulting social unrest in the poorer Mediterranean members of the eurozone and their conflict with the richer states have created unresolved political tensions.

The economic weaknesses and financial fragility of individual member states were exacerbated by the GFC, exposing the flaws of a stateless monetary system with a central bank that does not have sovereign power to create money. During the crisis, the most highly indebted states were not only in danger of default but also had insolvent banking systems on the brink of failure. The time-honoured solution of pumping money into the system, employed by the USA and the UK, was prevented by the strict terms of the Maastricht Treaty and the Growth and Stability Pact. The EU and European Monetary Union (EMU) were paralysed by their self-imposed rules in which there was no single body with the *discretionary* sovereign power to create the money to alleviate the debt and solvency crises (Ingham, 2004, 194–5; Otero-Iglesias, 2015). Member states' central banks were not permitted to create euros and the ECB was prohibited from purchasing EU member states' government bonds as a means of QE. In short, over a century after it had become standard practice in capitalism, there was no 'lender of last resort' in the eurozone.

The intensification of the effects of the GFC, which produced debt crises in Ireland, Greece, Spain, and Portugal, eventually led to significant departures from the definitive constituent elements of the eurozone system: that is, the strict separation of the monetary and fiscal domains and the creation of money to buy government debt. The prospect of the collapse of Greece's economy and its departure from the eurozone led the so-called 'troika' – the European Commission, the ECB, and the International Monetary Fund – to introduce a series of monetary 'bailouts' to enable the Greek government to meet interest payments on its debt to the bondholders. To maintain the formal integrity of the eurozone rules in the face of this blatant transgression, these were construed as an 'exceptional' measure in exchange for Greece's promise to restructure pensions and income tax and to introduce market reforms to 'liberalize' the economy. The episode clearly exposed the location of the euro's sovereign power in the unelected 'troika'.

Eventually, the effects of the GFC forced a further relaxation of the prohibition of the direct purchase of EU member states' government bonds by the ECB and a blurring of the separation of monetary and fiscal domains. Following QE in the USA and UK, the ECB embarked on similar indirect funding, which was done in a way that guaranteed profits for private banking and finance, maintaining the terms of the 'memorable alliance' between states and capital. The institutional mechanism for money creation by the contracting of debt on profitable terms to private capital was perfectly illustrated. After 2012, the ECB's state of 'exception' outside the democratic political realm enabled it to grant itself permission to create euros to purchase unlimited numbers of bonds issued by highly indebted EU governments at a fixed price. However, this was conditional on the prior purchase of the bonds from the member governments by private banks with money borrowed from their respective central banks.

The bonds were bought by the banks at a small discount – say, 95 per cent – and immediately resold to the ECB at a fixed price which guaranteed a profit of, say, 0.5 per cent (Streeck, 2014, 166).

The EMU was intended to provide a common currency for economic transactions in markets that were, in turn, intended to transcend the separate member states of the EU. Indeed, some believed that the liberal free trade policy, based on Smith's and Ricardo's 'classical' economics and its implicit theory of society, would eliminate conflict and competition between nation states. The longstanding rivalry between France and Germany would be overcome by the mutual benefits of economic interdependence.

Confidence in the viability of the eurozone project ultimately derives from economic models in which money is only a 'neutral' medium for the exchange of values created in the 'real' economy. In this conception, banking and financial crises are unfortunate aberrations, not systemic ever-present possibilities. Consequently, arrangements to resolve crises were not given priority in the blueprint for the single currency. The EU had not given the ECB the authority to act as a 'lender of last resort', but it could do so by exercising its 'exceptional' monetary sovereignty. In convoluted contortions aimed at disguising the departure from Maastricht, the ECB adopted this role *de facto* – if not *de jure*.

Of course, not all the *political* founders of the EMU were as convinced by economic theory's rationale for the euro. In 1991, the year before Maastricht, the German Chancellor, Helmut Kohl, told the Bundestag that 'history . . . teaches us that the idea of an economic and monetary union without a political union is a fallacy' (cited in Otero-Iglesias, 2015, 358). At this juncture in the late twentieth century, rivalry between member states precluded the logical way forward to political union; but the turmoil wrought by the GFC gave support to Kohl's judgement. In 2012, this was repeated by his successor as German Chancellor, Angela Merkel, who said that 'we need not only a monetary union, but we also need a so-called fiscal union, . . . we need most of all a political union – that means we need to gradually give competencies to Europe and give Europe control' (cited in Otero-Iglesias, 2015, 361). However, the arch-rivals Germany and France still cannot agree on the nature of a sovereign power that is necessary for European 'competencies' and 'control'. And if they do reach agreement, the weaker members fear the Franco-German dominance that might follow. Furthermore, the surge in populist nationalism has deterred many EU elites from pressing for pan-European political unification.

Conclusion

Aside from the eurozone, the creation of money in most modern capitalist states involves two sets of three-cornered relations. First, there is an institutional linkage – consisting of constitutional relationships, conventions, and accounting rules – between the state treasury, the central bank, and the franchise of regulated banks. Each produces money in the form of debt owed to them by their borrowers. The most important of the conventions governing these relationships are those which are intended to deter governments from using state sovereignty to create money for the direct financing of their expenditure ('monetization of debt'). This preserves the power and profitability of private capital in the money-creation process but compromises state monetary sovereignty. We shall see in chapter 7 that the GFC has revived the advocacy of democratic 'sovereign money', in which the power to create money would be removed from private banks.

The institutional mechanism and its conventions have been produced over time by struggles and tacit agreements between the main antagonists in the second of the three-cornered relationships: between the state expenditure; the state's bond-buying creditors, and the revenue from taxpayers for expenditure and interest payment on government debt. These complex and contradictory struggles dominate politics in modern democracies. On the one hand, for example, the state's creditors profit from their purchase of government debt, but at the same time fear that its growth might increase the possibility of default, posing a risk to their investments. On the other hand, however, they are ambivalent about the impact of any drastic reductions in government borrowing on the continuity of this safe lucrative investment opportunity.

Following President Clinton's intention to redeem US government debt in the 1990s, Federal Reserve Chairman Alan Greenspan had to placate the financial markets' concerns about the potential reduction of safe investment opportunities (Hager, 2016, 68). Increasing taxation to fund government debt is resisted by the electorate – especially, the wealthy creditor class, whose preferences prevail. In the USA and most probably elsewhere, there is a very high correlation over time between the top 1 per cent ownership of government debt and the top 1 per cent ownership of wealth (Hager, 2016, 41). Unease about the sudden large increase of government debt incurred by the bailout of the financial system in the GFC led to the introduction of 'austerity' in social welfare spending and public services rather than increased taxation to curb the debt.

In essence, monetary management in capitalism involves two 'balancing acts' in an uncertain world. First, money must be made scarce enough to avoid inflation and instability; but, at the same time, there must be enough money for *ex ante* financing of production and consumption by the creation of debt (Smithin, 2018). Currently, the production of this supply is shared: the largest single economic agent in capitalism – the state – *spends* it into existence; and the banking system *lends* it into existence. Second, this must be done in the face of the competing and conflicting claims of those who have an interest in how and how much money is produced: states, banks, debtors (including the state), and creditors (financiers and taxpayers). In chapter 7, we will return to questions raised about the efficiency, effectiveness, and legitimacy of these arrangements.

6

Modern Money (ii): 'Near' Money; 'Complementary', 'Alternative', and 'Surrogate' Money; and 'Crypto-Currency'

In addition to the money created by the state and franchised banks, most capitalist societies contain other means of payment that originate in smaller economic networks and local communities. Typically, these are found at each end of the economy. In the upper levels, capitalist financial enterprises issue their own promises of payment (IOUs) which circulate widely within relatively closed networks: that is, the 'near money' of the 'shadow' banks. As the term implies, these banks and their 'near' money exist alongside the state-regulated banking system in an opaque area of shifting and overlapping boundaries. They are the modern counterparts of the mercantile credit networks that grew in the early stages of capitalism. At lower levels, local communities and networks of small and medium-sized enterprises issue their own means of payment. In addition to these domestic moneys, there has been a proliferation of transnational crypto-currencies, based on blockchain technology and transmitted globally via the internet. By and large, a preponderance and proliferation of non-state moneys is inversely related to state power – especially, effective control of taxation. Weakening of state power can lead to an anarchic proliferation of 'alternative', 'complementary' forms of money, or of money 'surrogates' (commodities denominated in a money of account and used as payment).

'Near Money'

Capitalism's private property and contract law has ensured the continued existence of private acknowledgements of debt (IOUs) which by mutual agreement are accepted as payment in financial networks. In fact, as we have seen, most modern money is produced by the private–public partnership between the banking system and central bank by which privately contracted debt is transformed into public money. Strictly speaking, all bank money is 'private' at the point of issue and is often referred to in textbooks as 'inside' money, as opposed to 'outside' state money in the form of notes and coins.

Outside the monetary space of sovereign currency and the regulated banking system's franchised money, privately issued acknowledgements of debt/promises to pay (IOUs) circulate in financial networks as means of payment: 'commercial paper', 'certificates of deposit', 'bills of exchange', and so on. The 'liquidity', or 'nearness' to sovereign money, of these IOUs is determined by their degree of short-notice convertibility into it – either by the issuer or by a third party in the 'shadow' or 'secondary' banking network. This 'near money' is truly 'inside' today's relatively closed capitalist money and financial markets and is used in the same way as its early capitalist forerunners to short-circuit, or evade, the regulated banking and financial system.

The growth of 'inside' money and 'shadow' banking is closely associated with periods of rapid expansion and innovation in capitalist finance – especially, speculative booms in housing and stock markets. As the major locations of finance-capital, the UK and USA have experienced crises which were triggered by 'near' money's abrupt loss of liquidity caused by a chain reaction of issuers' defaults on their IOUs: for example, the UK's 'secondary banking crisis' in 1972. By far the largest expansion of 'near' money culminated in the GFC of 2008. Between 1995 and 2007 in the USA, privately issued financial sector IOUs grew from 54 per cent to 75 per cent of the total money supply, shrinking back again to 54 per cent by 2012 (Ricks, 2016, 35). Subsequently, the percentage has increased yet again in the USA and some other economies, particularly where 'socialism with Chinese characteristics' has unleashed 'shadow' banking on a vast, potentially destructive scale.

In very broad terms, half the total money supply in modern capitalism is privately issued 'inside' financial networks (Ricks, 2016). Consequently, governments and central banks have far less control of the monetary system than they would like and, indeed, claim to have. Their situation is a direct expression of the contradictory consequences of capitalism's hybrid public–private monetary and financial system. On the one hand, an attempt by states to reduce, or even prohibit, the issue of 'near' money in the money and financial markets would face fierce and powerful opposition, as shown by the dilution of the proposed reforms after the GFC (for a discussion of the control of private money, see Ricks 2016). Even if national radical reforms were enacted, they would most likely be rendered ineffective by global finance-capitalism. As we saw in the previous chapter, the exceptional government control of money after 1945 was possible because private capitalist finance had been unable fully to operate internationally during the war and had been temporarily subordinated in war finance and post-war reconstruction. This brief period of state power soon came to an end when global capitalism's 'normal service' was resumed.

Near' money involves a constant struggle between monetary authorities and private financial enterprise money creation. There is a recurrent tension in capitalist monetary systems as 'shadow' banks resist and evade regulation but clamour to be rescued from crises for which they are largely responsible. Attempts to impose tighter regulation of 'shadow' banks are often a largely ineffectual condition of the rescue.

However, although 'franchised' and 'near' private money creation by banks is a major factor in periodic crises, it has also been closely associated with economic growth throughout the history of capitalism. With the collapse of state socialism, almost all governments now see it as the only viable form of economic organization. The question of monetary reform and the role of privately issued money in the wake of the GFC will be considered in chapter 7, but we now turn to money creation at the other end of capitalism.

'Complementary', 'Alternative', and 'Surrogate' Money

Using force to consolidate the twin power bases of territory and taxation, states carve out co-extensive monetary and physical spaces, circumscribed by a single money of account and currency. These increasingly homogeneous and extensive monetary systems unintentionally laid the foundations for nationwide economic transactions. Large-scale, impersonal markets were superimposed on local community and regional markets, gradually displacing their local moneys (Fantacci, 2008). However, non-state moneys were never completely eliminated, and under certain circumstances 'complementary', 'alternative', and 'surrogate' moneys quickly reappeared alongside state money. It is estimated that over 5,000 such moneys exist across the world (North, 2007; Lietaer and Dunne 2013).

The different terms should not be taken precisely to identify distinct phenomena. They are inevitably used loosely, reflecting the complexity and fluidity of politically and economically unstable situations in which non-state moneys emerge. For example, transactions in urban Argentine communities can be conducted in complex combinations of state currency, local 'alternatives', and genuine barter of commodities (Saiag, 2019). None the less, it is useful to distinguish between 'complementary' and 'alternative'/'surrogate' money. Here, 'complementary' is used to refer to moneys that co-exist with but do not compete with the dominant state currency. 'Alternative' moneys arise in those situations where state money either has been rejected or is unavailable. In some cases, the state's money of account is replaced by an 'alternative' for denominating prices and debts. Despite the additional complexity, the term 'surrogate' makes it possible to make an important distinction between 'barter' and 'payment in kind' and to avoid an all too frequent confusion. Barter exchange of commodities, at a ratio agreed by the parties involved, does not involve a common money of account. Where commodities are used as payment after a state's currency has collapsed – for example, paint and electricity in Russia after 1991 – they are generally, but mistakenly, seen as barter. However, if the extant money of account is used to denominate prices and debts, goods accepted as 'payment in kind' are 'surrogates' for conventional means of payment. In Keynes's terms, the 'things' answering the 'description' of money have changed.

Complementary Currency

Local or regional complementary currencies are usually, but not exclusively, created to deal with economic depression. They seek to facilitate and maintain economic transactions by restricting money to its function as a *medium of exchange* in limited networks. The first widespread appearance of complementary non-state money in modern capitalism occurred during the inter-war Great Depression in Europe and the USA. In the USA between 1931 and 1935, hundreds of experimental local currencies were issued by various bodies for redemption in exchange for goods at local stores. In the main, they were short-lived and largely ineffective in improving economic conditions. However, US city governments' 'tax anticipation scrip' was more successful – enduring in some areas until the early 1940s. The depression had drastically cut local taxation revenue and cities met the shortfall by issuing their own credits, or 'scrip', which was used to pay employees and fund public services and, in turn, was accepted together with US dollars in payment of local taxes (Gatch, 2012).

In 1932, the city of Wörgl in Austria issued a currency (*Freigeld* – 'free money') based on the application of Silvio Gesell's monetary theory, which was favourably discussed by Keynes (Keynes, 1973 [1936]). To encourage spending rather than saving money as a store of value (Keynes's 'liquidity preference'), Gesell proposed that dated paper money should be stamped periodically with progressively deflated value (*demurrage*). The 'miracle of Wörgl', as it became known, was so successful in creating employment through new roads and housing that it attracted the attention of the Austrian central bank, which dealt with the threat to its power by prohibiting local currency. Unemployment returned to the town.

Although non-state moneys continue to be used to counter local economic deprivation, 'complementary' currencies also emerged during the late twentieth century in affluent regions of advanced economies – perhaps as a communitarian response to globalization. The origin of modern grassroots 'complementary' money is widely attributed to a computer-based 'local exchange trading scheme' (LETS) set up by Michael Linton in Vancouver, Canada, in 1983. The software enabled participants to communicate their offers and wants and record their credits and debits in terms of a common unit of exchange. LETS spread rapidly across advanced and developing societies, using paper, collection boxes, and the internet for posting and clearing credits and debits. Units of account for the transactions usually shadow the national currency, sometimes assuming a local identity, such as Canterbury 'Tales' and Manchester 'Bobbins' in the UK.

Strictly speaking, LETS are barter-credit networks in so far as currency for further trading can only be acquired by offers of goods and services by network participants. This allows a separation of transactions in time, overcoming the limitation of the 'absence of a double coincidence of wants' in direct bilateral barter. By shadowing the mainstream nominal currency, participants can post a price for their goods and services which resolves the problem of the absence of a unit of account in barter. In this way, a level of multilateral exchange is achieved, but the media of exchange remain firmly embedded in a network based on continuous preparedness to trade. Hoarding would impede the continuity of exchange and is actively discouraged in some systems by *demurrage*. Therefore, unlike the disembedded money in the mainstream economy, LETS media cannot be dissociated from transactions to become abstract stores of value for use as unilateral settlement of monetary debt. Furthermore, LETS media of exchange are not backed by an issuer's promise to accept them in payment for any debt owed – as in taxation. This is money as 'a mere intermediary, without significance in itself, which flows from one hand to another, is received and is dispensed, and disappears when its work is done' (Keynes, 1971 [1923], 124).

If a separate money of account is adopted, 'complementary' currency often becomes an 'alternative' to the mainstream money, which is unattainable owing to high levels of unempioyment or unavailable owing to shortages. In Argentina, the crédito replaced the national peso as a unit of account in many of the exchange networks (*trueques*) which have expanded and contracted in response to economic conditions and monetary crises over the past thirty years. Credits and debits denominated in créditos are issued to participants to be used in exchange networks centred on local markets (*feria*) in urban areas. By enabling local economic and social projects, some 'alternative' créditos have become symbolic expressions of communal and political solidarity.

Argentina presents an exceptional case of a modern developed state in which a plurality of 'alternative' currencies has existed to varying degrees and at all levels since the late nineteenth century. In addition to grassroots créditos, Argentine provincial governments have issued their own currencies (bonos) periodically over many years to pay employees and suppliers. The provincial issue is accepted in payment of local taxation, giving the currency value and inaugurating a stable fiscal cycle of employment–taxation– expenditure. Indeed, it has been argued that the currency issued in Tucuman is more stable than the national currency (Théret, 2017).

Some 'complementary' currencies have the potential to move out of their original 'embedded' network by promising convertibility with the mainstream currency: for example, 'Brixton pounds' in the UK and 'SoNantes' in Nantes, France. An incentive to use these local convertible currencies is given by favourable/unfavourable exchange rates for buying/selling local currency. For example, until the end of 2013, £100 in UK pounds would buy £110 in Brixton pounds; conversely, £100 in Brixton pounds exchanged for £90 in UK pounds. If local 'complementary' currencies do not diminish tax revenue or challenge control of the monetary system, they are tolerated by modern states and, in some cases, actively encouraged in the pursuit of economic welfare and employment.

Advances in information and communication technology have made it possible to develop large and extensive online credit networks ('closed loop' payment systems) between enterprises in economically depressed regions. For example, the Sardex network in Sardinia, which is supported by the

EU, is a clearing mechanism for transactions that enables participating enterprises with a cash shortage to continue to operate. Its impact is limited, however, accounting for less than 1 per cent of Sardinia's GDP (Lucarelli and Gobbi, 2016, 1416).

'Complementary' currency is widely advocated by otherwise opposed ideological camps as a means of escaping or countering the overweening control of the modern state (North, 2007; Dodd, 2014, chaps 7–8) For economic liberals, the emergence of non-state money is evidence for the Hayekian free market theory of money. At the other end of the ideological spectrum, 'complementary' currency is seen as a means of fostering and expressing communal solidarity. Indeed, many schemes are explicitly intended primarily to generate social solidarity by empowering local communities to unlock the 'real' wealth, or social capital, residing in their skills and enterprise (see Dodd, 2014, 342). Some proposals today are closely associated with anti-state, anti-capitalist, and anti-globalization movements. It is believed that communal money could counter and transform despotic bank and state power – a truly 'social technology' for improving human welfare, controlled by its users in a truly democratic society.

Crypto-Currencies

Information technology has also been used to create an entirely novel form of money. Crypto-currencies are expressly intended to be an alternative to state money, but in sharp contrast to community-based currencies, they are not embedded in a local social and economic network. On the contrary, one of the intentions behind Bitcoin's launch in 2009 was to remove money entirely from its social and political foundations. This has been followed by Ethereum, Litecoin, Ripple, and many others, which by 2018 totalled over 1,500 (*www. coinmarketcap.com*).

Crypto-currencies do not simply use computer software and information technology to transmit money electronically to and from bank deposits in 'online banking'. Rather, the money itself is cryptographically located in the very software

– blockchain technology – by which it is produced. Blockchain is a series of records of crypto-currency creation and transactions, or 'chains', forming a 'block'. Secure encryption ensures that traders and owners of currency cannot modify the files governing its creation. Scarcity of currency is built into the programs: for example, no more than 21 million Bitcoins will ever exist. These are acquired by being 'mined', using complex algorithms on 'application-specific' PCs with vast computing power, and then stored in digital 'wallets' in cyberspace. As more 'miners' become involved in acquiring crypto-currency, computation increases in complexity, requiring very expensive multiple high-performance computers. Before its surge in value, Bitcoin scarcely justified the expenditure on setting up the machines, the electricity required to run them, and the air conditioning to deal with the enormous amount of heat produced.

Three claims were made for the superiority of Bitcoin over conventional money. First, the finite supply built into the encryption is analogous to the natural scarcity of gold, pre-empting credit bubbles caused by the potentially unlimited supply of state fiat money and bank-created deposits. In the words of Satoshi Nakamoto, the pseudonym of the individual or group who devised the Bitcoin scheme,

> The root problem with conventional currency is all the trust that's required to make it work. The central bank must be trusted not to debase the currency, but the history of fiat currencies is full of breaches of that trust. Banks must be trusted to hold our money, but they lend it out in waves of credit bubbles with barely a fraction in reserve. (*http://p2pfoundation.ning.com/forum/topics/bitcoin-open-source*)

Ironically, this has been precisely Bitcoin's fate together with myriad other 'alt-currencies' that have been devised to take advantage of speculation on their rapidly rising price. At the peak of the 'crypto-mania' during 2017, several hundred currencies with a market value of over $80 billion were listed on several exchanges. As in the South Sea Bubble craze of 1720, which featured a stock prospectus for 'a company for carrying out an undertaking of great advantage, but nobody to know what it is', some speculators found themselves in possession of claims to currencies that never existed. By 2017, Bitcoin's dollar exchange rate had risen rose from $106 in 2013 to $19,000 before the bubble burst in December, sending the price down to $7,000 by April 2018. A gradual slide has followed to $4,000 by November 2018 followed by a slight recovery to over $5,000 in May 2019.

A second claim that secure encryption ensured that Bitcoin was safer than mainstream banking and conventional currency was dashed by the collapse of Mt Gox and other crypto-currency exchanges. Based in Tokyo and launched in July 2010, Mt Gox was handling over 70 per cent of all worldwide transactions at the time trading was suspended in February 2014. Hackers broke into the exchanges' encrypted 'wallets' and 'ledgers' and stole around 850,000 Bitcoins, valued at more than $450 million. Subsequently, Bitfinex, CoinCheck, and other exchanges have been penetrated by 'Trojan Horse' computer programs which have looted their 'ledgers'.

Thirdly, it was claimed that unlike the deposits of named account holders in conventional internet banking, securely encrypted ownership of the currency was as anonymous as state-issued cash, making it useful in illegal trade on the 'dark web' and criminal networks. However, FBI investigations have shattered confidence in Bitcoin's anonymity. In 2015, Ross Ulbricht, the American creator of the $1 billion Silk Road drugs market, which was underpinned by Bitcoin, was sentenced to life in prison. Later the same year, the organizer of a $150 million crypto-currency Ponzi scheme was charged with fraud and a former Mt Gox employee was charged with embezzling $390 million of Bitcoins from the exchange. Again, ironically, the trail of data associated with illegal trading can be traced using similarly powerful information technology. These security failures have cast doubt on the much vaunted forecasts of 'end of cash' and its replacement by blockchain monetary technology, administered by central banks.

Apart from a short period after its introduction, crypto-currency has proved unable to perform money's basic functions. The extreme volatility of Bitcoin's exchange-value has made it unsuitable as a money of account for pricing commodities and unacceptable as a means of payment. Rather, it has become the latest in a long line of capitalism's speculative 'manias', which began with tulips in mid-seventeenth-century

Holland. 'Initial coin offerings' of crypto-currency are now made exclusively on expectations of a rise in their value. The volatility has attracted the attention of derivatives markets offering contracts on future prices and the emergence of 'shorting', in which speculators offer to sell crypto-currencies at a higher price than the one they subsequently hope to buy them for. Crypto-currency does precisely what money should *not* do: that is, introduce uncertainty into transactions. There is reluctance to use it as a means of payment for fear of losing a possible large increase in exchange-value; but, conversely, an equally probable loss of value may deter acceptance on the part of the seller.

Conclusion

Large claims are made for how information technology might transform money and society, liberating us from the centralized domination of the modern state. This common stance, found at each end of the broad political spectrum, can be traced to the implications of the two fundamentally different general theories of social order that we encountered earlier. On the one hand, the relative ease with which the internet and information technology enable the proliferation of non-state currency is seen to confirm that the 'market', comprising otherwise 'isolated' utility-maximizing individuals, is the basic unit of society (see the discussion of 'market isolation' in Orléan, 2014a). On the other hand, it is widely believed that local 'complementary' currency, based on the same information technology, could unlock latent skills to counter unemployment and economic deprivation, revitalizing 'social capital' and social solidarity lying dormant in all communities. Some take these possibilities further and envisage the triumph of the local over the global, the community over the state, and cooperation over monopoly capitalism. With non-state media of exchange, '[t]he sheer volume, speed and spatial dispersion of . . . transactions will ultimately defeat the revenue collecting bureaucracies . . . [T]he territorial dimension of society will devolve to more local units' (Hart, 2000, 316; see the discussion of money and 'utopia' in Dodd, 2014, chap. 8).

However, recent history has shown the limitations of both 'market' and 'community' money and, by implication, the shortcomings of the underlying theories of money and social order on which they are based. 'Market' theories of money, following Hayek, hold that stable money will emerge from rational choices between myriad competing currencies and, by implication, that social order is produced by recognition of the advantages of interdependence for the pursuit of self-interest. However, competition between the exchange-values of an increasing number of crypto-currencies has produced the bubble and instability that the market was supposed to eliminate. To be sure, local money can help to generate communal trust and economic activity, but there is no foundation for thinking that it could ever be more than 'a complement' to a viable mainstream currency and become the basis for socialist or communitarian society. Despite the ideological opposition to the market exchange theory of social order, these 'utopian' schemes imply the same – somewhat contradictory – underlying theory of money. On the one hand, both view money itself as the active means by which their respective 'vision' of a social order could be realized independently of a centralized state. On the other hand, both see money merely as a reflection or passive expression of the 'real' values created in economic exchange and the 'real' social forces inherent in communal solidarity.

However, money is a 'social technology' that has enabled the construction of large-scale social systems from Babylon to the present. Money performs most effectively as the means of coordinating complex transactions when the question of trust is detached from those directly involved and is transferred to the issuer. This replaces personal trust with the impersonal trust that enables exchange between strangers across time and space. Money makes markets. It is significant that the most successful and enduring local currencies in Argentina have not been those in the communal *trueques* but the créditos issued by provincial governments acting as 'mini-sovereign states' in a loose monetary federalism.

State monopoly of coercion and the gradual dissipation of general violence in society is the ultimate foundation for a large-scale society and viable money. Furthermore, this perspective allows us to see more clearly that money is more than a mere medium of exchange and means of payment. The successful establishment of Mirowski's 'working fiction of an invariant standard' is a precondition for the continuity of social and economic order.

7
The Great Financial Crisis and the Question of Money

On 5 November 2008, when opening a new building at the London School of Economics, Queen Elizabeth II drew attention to academic economics by asking why none of the distinguished practitioners had foreseen the GFC. How could complex mathematical models have failed to detect any signs of such an event? Goldman Sachs's Chief Financial Officer, David Viniar, was ridiculed for the answer he gave to the US Senate Committee in April 2011. The crisis was unforeseeable because according to the models it consisted of events of 'twenty-five standard-deviation points several days in a row'. Statisticians flocked to point out that even one such twenty-five standard-deviation point event was unlikely to occur in the entire history of the universe. Did this mean that the models were telling Viniar that the financial crisis had not happened (Authers, 2017)?

In response to a similar question at the same time, Larry Summers – former Chief Economist at the World Bank and ex-Director of President Obama's National Economic Council – bluntly explained that the 'vast edifice of economic theory constructed since the Second World War had been virtually useless' because money and finance were excluded as independent variables from central banks' models (cited in Martin 2013, 190; see also Buiter, 2009; Ingham, 2011; Turner, 2016; King, 2017). Consequently, the models foreclosed any possible anticipation of the GFC. Mervyn King,

Governor of the Bank of England during the crisis, agreed: '[M]y experience at the Bank ... revealed the inadequacy of the "models" ... used by economists to explain swings in total spending and production. In particular, such models say nothing about the importance of money and banks and the panoply of financial markets that feature prominently in newspapers and on our television screens' (King, 2017, 7). Most contributors to the 'vast edifice of economic theory' were probably unaware that the assumption of a constant value of 'neutral' money had its origins in an anachronistic concept of the economy as a quasi-barter system in which one commodity 'buys' all others but has no impact on their production or fluctuations in economic activity.

On a more practical level, as in all serious monetary and financial crises, the events of 2008 stimulated a wide range of proposals to prevent a recurrence. On the one hand, governments inaugurated investigations which, as usual, reported that the existing system was fundamentally sound, but required tighter regulation and a little restructuring. In the USA, for example, Paul Volcker, Chair of President Obama's Economic Recovery Advisory Board, argued that that banks and financial institutions should hold more reserves and capital; and, more controversially, he recommended the reintroduction of the separation of investment from deposit banking, introduced following the 1930s crises. The Glass–Steagall Act (1933) had sought to protect savers' deposits from being used in riskier investment banking but had been repealed in 1999. The Vickers Commission in the UK proposed a weaker version that would 'ring-fence' the two types of banking within the existing banks. Despite the mild officially sponsored recommendations for piecemeal reforms, bankers in the USA none the less embarked on vigorous and successful opposition to Volcker's proposals – especially the separation of investment and deposit banking. The view that the GFC was not systemic but caused by human failings and dishonest 'bad apples' was received more favourably. With displays of contrition, bankers wholeheartedly agreed to a change of 'culture' whereby greed and excessive risk-taking would be replaced by an ethos of service to society.

None the less, for a while, more critical analyses of money and capitalism were widely and openly discussed. As we saw in chapter 3, the GFC was dubbed a 'Minsky moment', in reference to the largely ignored heterodox economist Hyman Minsky, who had argued that financial crises were normal events in capitalism (Minsky, 1982). Banking's transformation of private debt into public money is the source of capitalism's dynamism *and* fragility. This method for funding both production and financial speculation inevitably carries the possibility of a chain reaction of defaults followed by economic disruption. Debt financing of production leads to unstable oscillations between speculative expansion and 'overproduction', followed by 'debt deflation' and stagnation when demand is exhausted. After governments dropped their commitment to Keynes's prescriptions in the 1970s (see chapter 4), 'aggregate demand' was subsequently financed by consumer debt – in effect, by 'privatized Keynesianism' (Crouch, 2009). Governments encouraged the energetic marketing of mortgage debt to create a 'property-owning democracy', which led to a series of expansionary 'booms' and 'busts', culminating in the 'sub-prime' crisis in 2007 (Ingham, 2011). And, of course, periodic economic instability continues in markets for financial assets with the inevitable bursting of speculative 'bubbles'.

Two general questions were posed in a large and diverse critical literature (Wolf, 2014 and Turner, 2016 give comprehensive accessible accounts). First, as the source of the fuel for stoking crises, should the banking system's capacity to create money be more strictly controlled or even removed? Second, should the money-creating power of 'unelected' central banks be more accountable (Pixley, 2018; Tucker, 2018)? Both at least implied fundamental questions about where the creation, control, and management of money should be located in modern democracies.

Controlling the Money-Creating Bank Franchise

In 1933, a group of Chicago economists identified the easy creation of bank credit money as the underlying cause of the 1929 Wall Street Crash and subsequent chain reaction of debt defaults, bank failures, deflation, and depression. They submitted a plan to President Roosevelt in 1933 proposing that all banks should hold 100 per cent reserves at the central bank, which would eliminate the production of money by the creation of deposits for borrowers that were unmatched by existing reserves. If implemented, banks would have been restricted to making payments between accounts and acting as intermediaries between savers and borrowers. Aware that capitalism required the prior introduction of purchasing power to ensure that production and consumption took place, the Chicago economists recommended that governments ran small deficits funded by their creation of fiat money. This would replace the need to borrow from private capital by the sale of interest-bearing bonds (see chapter 5).

The 'Chicago Plan' for full reserve banking (FRB) was not adopted, but, following the GFC, its revival by International Monetary Fund economists was widely reported in the media (for example, Benes and Kumhof, 2012). This and similar proposals were given serious reconsideration by influential commentators such as Martin Wolf, Chief Economics Correspondent of the *Financial Times* (Wolf, 2014), and Adair Turner, former Chairman of the UK's Financial Services Authority (Turner, 2016). The UK think-tank Positive Money (Dyson et al., 2016), for example, advanced a scheme arguing that the banks' power to create money should be removed and replaced entirely by government 'sovereign money', which would be 'debt-free' in that governments would not need to be funded by selling interest-bearing bonds. (Of course, money can never be 'debt-free' in the sense that its acceptability is based on the issuer's promise to accept it in payment of any debt owed – see Nersisyan and Wray, 2016.)

Central banks, it was argued, should be given the exclusive control of money creation but lose their 'independence', pursuing objectives of economic policy as set by governments. This would allow a change of direction in the flow of money away from financial speculation and commercial property and into production and employment. Furthermore, with digital currency, everyone could have an account at the central bank, which would greatly enhance the administration and control of the money supply (for example, Huber, 2017; Moe, 2018). In addition to eliminating the lax control and ill-direction of money, disestablishing the money-creating franchise would remove the banks' seigniorage profits: that is, their ability to 'make money from making money' (Macfarlane et al., 2017). Mainstream academic finance and economics largely ignored these initiatives, which were rejected as 'cranky' even by heterodox economist critics of bank power. (For an academic discussion and critiques of FRB, 'sovereign money', and similar proposals, see Ingham et al., 2016; Pettifor, 2017). Critics raised three main objections.

First, lending and borrowing might be too restrictive to meet investment if it were entirely in the hands of the central bank. Some suggested that a national investment bank should be established.

Second, the creation of non-state money would not be eliminated by the control or abolition of the licensed regulated banks' franchise. Indeed, any restrictions on this sector would stimulate an expansion of 'shadow' banking's 'near money' and 'cash equivalents' to meet the demand for money. Furthermore, in an important contribution, Morgan Ricks has identified the vast expansion of money in 'shadow' banking – not the franchised licensed sector – as the major cause of the GFC and other 'bubbles' (Ricks, 2016). Here, the problem is not so much loosely controlled bank lending and consequent chain reactions of default, but the proliferation of inherently fragile privately issued IOUs in financial networks (see chapter 5). Unlike the deposits created by the bank franchise, 'near money' is not covered by deposit insurance and underwriting by the central bank. Consequently, the liquidity, or 'cash equivalence', of 'near' money – that is, its acceptability and exchangeability for state money – is entirely dependent on the precarious creditworthiness of the private issuers. In 2007, the problem was not so much that default was the simple result of insolvency: that is, when debts are not matched by assets. Rather, inability to make payment within the financial system was caused – or, at least, greatly exacerbated – by the rapidly increasing widespread illiquidity of 'near money'. Without the probability that IOUs were exchangeable for sovereign money ('cash equivalent'), financial networks disintegrated and dislocation spread to the regulated banking system. The utter uncertainty about both lenders' and borrowers' solvency led to the 'credit crunch': that is, an almost complete reluctance to lend. The obvious solution to this source of systemic fragility in the monetary system would be to prohibit the use of privately issued IOUs. However, as we have noted, this would involve changes to the contract law that underpins capitalism. Ricks believes that despite political obstacles, governments have the power to prohibit all 'shadow' banking. None the less, he shares the conventional belief that decentralized 'lending' rather than centralized government 'spending' is better able to allocate money more efficiently. Governments and their licensed banking sector should collaborate more closely (see the discussion in Moe, 2018).

Third, as Ann Pettifor has acutely observed, 'sovereign money' proposals share the same mistaken focus as the old orthodox 'quantity theory' on monetary policy as the calculation of a non-inflationary *supply* of money in relation to forecast production. She quotes Keynes's 'Open Letter to President Roosevelt' (1933) at the time of the 'Chicago Plan', in which he pointed out that although reducing the money supply can curb economic activity, it was fallacious to infer that the converse is true. Merely increasing the *supply* of money to raise output and income was 'like trying to get fat by buying a larger belt . . . "the volume of *expenditure*" rather than the *quantity* of money "is the *operative* force"' (quoted in Pettifor, 2017, 98, emphasis added; see also Skidelsky 2018). Moreover, exclusive control of the money supply by a Money Creation Committee, as proposed or implied by the advocates of 'sovereign money', would increase the concentration of 'unelected' power in the monetary system.

Following Keynes's identification of the demand for money expenditure as the effective force, Pettifor believes that this would be best served by a balanced and non-exploitative relationship between creditors (bankers) and debtors (borrowers) in a 'socially just monetary system' (Pettifor, 2017, 112). Of course, this begs all the questions – as also do the schemes criticized by Pettifor. For example, Positive Money tends to assume that those placed in control of the government's 'sovereign money' would share their political and economic aims. Moreover, a 'socially just monetary system' might involve all manner of changes to how money is created and deployed, but it has first to be constructed. At the very least, this objective presupposes the kind of balance of power and social democratic settlement that occurred after 1945, during which time the Bank of England was brought into public ownership if not public control (on central banks and democracy, see Pixley, 2018).

Central Banks: 'Unelected' Power

In chapter 5, we saw that saving the banks after the GFC checked the disintegration of capitalism's vast networks of debt and prevented stagnation and depression (see Ingham, 2011, Postscript). After the government's authorization of £500 billion to thaw the frozen financial system in the UK, the Governor of the Bank of England, Mervyn King, wittily reversed Winston Churchill's judgement of the Battle of Britain in 1940: '[N]ever in the field of financial endeavour has so much been owed by so few to so many.' Together with many others, King was drawing attention to the public ('the many') subvention of private profit-making ('the few'), which came more sharply into focus when it was decided that this should be funded by large and protracted reduction of government expenditure. After the creation of enormous sums of money for the rescue, followed by QE, the insistence that immediate 'austerity' measures were necessary was met with scepticism. The banks might well be 'too big to fail', but presenting the decisions to save them, swelling the banks' reserves, and in effect asking the public to pay for it all provoked critical examinations of established procedures for creating money (for example, Wolf, 2014; Turner, 2016; Skidelsky, 2018, chap. 9).

The consequences of QE added more force to the questioning of central bank 'independence' and the 'neutrality' of money. It became apparent that QE had failed in one of its aims (see chapter 5). The increase in banks' reserves to maintain the downward pressure on interest rates had eased governments' debt burdens but had not stimulated investment in production and employment. Furthermore, QE had a perverse unintended consequence of increasing inequality. The central bank's creation of money to repurchase government bonds from the banks, originally purchased by them with central bank money created for that purpose, increased demand for bonds, driving up their price. Bondholders' wealth was increased and invested in other assets to avoid the very low rates of interest on bank deposits. Consequently, stock markets have boomed; the prices of houses, classic luxury cars, wine, and fine art have soared; and markets in riskier assets such as crypto-currencies have flourished. Furthermore, with their secure collateral, the wealthy can take advantage of the low interest rates to borrow for investment in these assets. Keynes's demand that governments should do what capitalists were not doing – that is, spend on productive investment – assumed renewed relevance (Turner, 2016, chap. 7; Skidelsky, 2018).

Questions were posed and proposals were made. First, if unelected central bank functionaries could create money to refinance private banks and – albeit unintentionally – enrich the financial plutocracy, why could they not do the same to deal with housing crises and disintegrating public infrastructure? Why could there not be a 'People's QE'? Despite the radical and democratic intentions, merely posing the question presupposes that the political question of how and by whom money is created has been resolved. Without significant institutional change, the control of money will stay with the 'independent' central bank, further enhancing the power of unelected technocrats (see the discussion in Pettifor, 2017, 117–28; see also the extensive discussion in former Bank of England official Paul Tucker's *Unelected Power*, 2018).

QE also drew attention to the central bank's role in the conventional labyrinthine procedure for money creation by the sale and repurchase of treasury bonds from private capital. Surely, it would be more efficient for the government and/ or the central bank simply to inject money directly into the economy? With digital money technology, it would not be necessary to scatter banknotes from 'helicopters', as Milton Friedman suggested in his 1960s thought-experiment (for a discussion, see Turner, 2016, 218-22). Almost the entire population could have money placed electronically at their disposal. However, as Keynes argued, an increase in the quantity of money would not necessarily lead to productive investment. His characteristically ironic conjecture pointed also to the political nub of the issue: that is, the conventional relationship between the state and private capital. To implement a monetary stimulus that conformed to 'the well-tried principles of laissez-faire', the Treasury should 'fill old bottles with banknotes, bury them . . . in disused coal mines . . . and leave it to private enterprise . . . to dig the notes up again' (Keynes, 1973 [1936], 129). Of course, as Keynes added, a more sensible solution would be for governments to build houses: that is, to ensure that the money was effectively spent; but, as he recognized, further political difficulties would stand in the way. In other words, it is not a technical question of *how* to create money but of *who* should do so and to what ends. Any move towards implementing the proposals in the critiques would require not only institutional change but also a counter-revolution in the hegemonic economic theory.

The economic failure and unintended consequences of QE added weight to more fundamental questions about the 'new macroeconomic consensus', based on a critique of Keynesian economics, which has informed government policy in the major economies since the 1990s (see chapter 5; Skidelsky, 2016, 196-9). The primary objective is monetary stability – that is, the elimination of inflation and inflation expectations – which, it is argued, will allow rational agents and the supply-and-demand mechanism to move towards equilibrium. For example, as we noted in chapter 3, the 'rational expectations' critique of Keynesian economics claimed to refute the effectiveness of fiscal policy in stimulating the economy with increased public expenditure. The priority of monetary over fiscal policy had been established and institutionalized in the location of money power in ostensibly independent central banks which would adjust interest rates to achieve non-inflationary growth. However, the limits of relying exclusively on monetary policy were now exposed. With near-zero interest rates, central banks could no longer influence banking systems' 'endogenous' creation of deposits of money with interest rate cuts to encourage borrowing – as they had done since 'monetarism' was abandoned in the late twentieth century. The only measure left to increase the potential supply of money was by the indirect QE of the banks' reserves; consequently, 'willy nilly central bankers became quantity theorists' (Skidelsky, 2018, 256).

Leaving aside the disputes about the technical efficacy of the different proposals for monetary reform and direct injection of money into the economy, they display to varying degrees a level of optimistic naïvety about the politics of money. As we have seen, the creation of money is the result of centuries of political and ideological development in which economic 'science' played an important part. Counterintuitively, however, the question of money cannot be solved by starting with money itself. In this regard, both mainstream monetary economics and their heterodox critics tend to *hypostasize* money (Cartelier, 2007); see also chapter 3): that is, to imply that changes in the theoretical understanding of money and in its forms and technology of transmission are the most important consideration.

To be sure, credit and state theories see money as a socially created power, but even here the focus on money itself can lead to a neglect of the essential political conditions for monetary reform. In this regard, for example, it has been suggested that MMT's analysis and proposals are more applicable to the USA, where the global strength of the dollar makes it less vulnerable to attacks from the bond markets. As things stand, the dollar and US government bonds are the ultimate safe haven for international investors, who would be less inclined to sell them off in response to an unfavourable assessment of government spending than they would be if they belonged to weaker states. The advocacy of 'sovereign money', by Positive Money and others, as a public resource to be administered by a 'money creation committee' presupposes – at the very least – a political consensus of the kind that occurred briefly and temporarily after 1945 (see chapter 4). Otherwise, any such arrangement would exhibit the same lack of legitimacy and accountability as the current central bank expert technocracy (Pettifor, 2017).

A decade after the GFC, the question of monetary reform is fading from view, where it will remain until the next big crisis and possibly a more serious examination of the political foundations of money. When this debate re-emerges, there will be some unfinished business to attend to, for whereas technical discussions of FRB and other monetary reforms were revived after the GFC, a slightly earlier but equally pertinent debate on the possibility of 'socialist money' was surprisingly neglected (Turner, 2016, 248–51 is an exception).

Democratic or Socialist Money?

Could there be truly democratic money? By what means might a public agency reach an agreement on the principles and management of the supply of money – how much and to what ends? Of course, these are distinctly *political* questions, and we have emphasized that money questions can never be simply a matter of technical economics. But it would be mistaken to conclude that money is *exclusively* political: that is, that given the 'correct' theory of money and the right political will, we are free to create monetary systems in any way we wish.

Early twentieth-century socialists went much further than our recent moderate critics. As the source of capitalist exploitation and recurring speculative crises, would money even be necessary in a socialist or truly democratic society? In the absence of classes and class conflict, there would be a universal agreement on collective economic goals. Consequently, the anarchy of market-determined prices could be replaced by a centrally planned equilibration of supplies of money and commodities, eliminating instability. This optimism proved to be as misplaced as the belief that the rational pursuit of self-interest in the free market would produce the same outcome. These two utopian visions of the economy contain two fundamentally different answers to questions about the systemic relationships between money, information, calculation, and uncertainty. Do the functions and operation of viable and effective money require specific institutional arrangements that limit and constrain how it can be created? Could a complex advanced economy operate without money?

Conventional academic economic and finance theory implies an affirmative answer to the first question. The ways in which money is currently produced and organized are by and large tried and tested. Modern monetary and financial systems are the result of 'evolutionary selection' in which increasingly efficient practices are sequentially adopted – aided by academic economics. Perfection may never be attained, but 'design faults' can be incrementally remedied: for example, the universal adoption of central banks as 'lenders of last resort'. Although, as we have argued, the capitalist monetary system was produced by a sequence of historical compromises between competing interests (see chapter 4), this is not to say that the institutions contingently created in this way have necessarily impeded efficiency and effectiveness.

Undoubtedly, there is a concentration of political and economic power in capitalist monetary systems, but they are not monolithic like those of the ancient empires and the twentieth century's defunct communist states. Money in capitalism remains relatively decentralized, comprising money creation shared between states and licensed banks; independent central banks; 'shadow' banks; 'near' money; and myriad 'complementary' and 'alternative' currencies. Does this complexity, conflict, and competition provide the diversity, flexibility, and innovation from which effective and efficient solutions to problems are generated and selected?

These questions arose in a slightly different guise during the early twentieth century in the 'socialist calculation debate' (for a survey, see Boettke, 2000; Levy and Peart, 2008). Socialists correctly identified money as the basic element in the capitalist dynamic of producing commodities for their exchange-value and for the calculation of profit. With the concentration of economic power in finance-capitalism, this dynamic was the source of exploitation, conflict, speculation, and instability. Aside from utopian schemes for the abolition of money, it was widely believed that monetary calculation could be replaced by *calculation in kind* in a socialist economy. Commodities would be produced for their agreed *use-values*, which could be calculated by valuing resources in terms of their relative quantitative contributions to production: most notably, for example, in Marx's 'labour theory of value', in which 'labour time' is both the ultimate source and measure of value. (Readers will note that, paradoxically, this bears a close relationship to 'bourgeois' classical economics' concept of the 'real' economy, discussed earlier. See Smithin, 2018, 71-4 on Marx's Ricardian heritage.)

Otto Neurath, an adviser to the short-lived Bavarian Soviet Republic (1918–19) that appeared during the revolutionary founding of Weimar Germany, argued that the organization of war production provided a blueprint for a socialist economy that could dispense with money prices by being physically planned. Instead, the functional contributions of physical magnitudes of disaggregated forces of production could be calculated: for example, a greater quantity of labour might increase output more than, say, increased use of electricity.

The reply by Ludwig von Mises in 'Economic Calculation in the Socialist Commonwealth', later elaborated by Friedrich Hayek, argued that in a world of uncertainty and irremediably imperfect information, we can never have enough foresight and knowledge effectively to plan an economy. Bureaucratic or technocratic methods cannot possibly acquire all the necessary information to allocate resources rationally. Economic rationality is best achieved by adaptive trial-and-error responses to money prices produced by the 'invisible hand' of decentralized markets. Without this monetary calculation, '[t]he human mind cannot orient itself properly among the bewildering mass of intermediate products and potentialities of production. It would simply stand perplexed' (von Mises, 1990 [1920], 13).

Some socialist responses to the critique accepted that it would be necessary to use money, rather than physical or engineering criteria, to measure and calculate the value of commodities and means of production. The Polish economist Oskar Lange, writing in the 1930s, proposed a model in which state-owned firms would be instructed by a central planning authority to fix prices in relation to marginal cost. In turn, the planning authority, using these prices, would be able by trial and error to arrive at prices where supply and demand were in equilibrium. Some believed that simultaneous equations could replace the planners' trial and error. Planners in these models are in effect a 'surrogate market', but as the means of production are publicly owned, this and similar models became known as 'market socialism'. (Again, the reader will note that these models were essentially the same as those in modern 'bourgeois' economics, based on Walras's 'general equilibrium', in which an 'auctioneer' sets prices with a *numeraire*.)

In principle, vastly increased computing power has made large-scale planning more feasible and has led to the revival of these ideas. In their book *People's Republic of Walmart*, Leigh Phillips and Michal Rozworksi contend that central planning in today's multinational corporations is 'laying the foundation for socialism' (Phillips and Rozworski, 2019).

Does Amazon present a possible socialist future? Aside from other problems – such as the fact that large centrally planned enterprises have always been a core element in monopoly capitalism – this conjecture must also confront von Mises's and Hayek's knowledge and information problem, which was so evident in the failed communist economic systems (Woodruff, 1999; Devine, 2010; Ellman, 2014). Moreover, even if the technical economic problems were to be resolved, the fundamental political question remains of how democratic or socialist politics might best be achieved. Indeed, as some critics of monetary reform have insisted, unless this is more clearly specified, any socialist central control of money will entail a contradictory concentration of power.

Max Weber made a sophisticated and distinctively different contribution to the debate which doesn't focus on the technical economic and information problems. Rather, his emphasis on the political nature of money as 'a weapon in the struggle for economic existence' led him to draw conclusions on the possible limits to radical monetary reform. Do the functions and operation of viable and effective money require definite institutional arrangements that limit and constrain how it can be created?

Writing before the advent of centrally planned economies, but informed by knowledge of ancient empires and an acute sociological analysis, Weber anticipated the difficulties that they were to experience. In his analysis of capitalism, he distinguished *capital accounting* – the calculation of *profitability* by competing enterprises – from *budgetary calculation* – the arbitrary assigning of monetary values for the internal management of resources. He believed that the capitalist calculation of profitability was a superior method for enabling the efficient use of resources, but it could only be pursued rationally by the ex-post calculation of costs and revenues represented by 'effective' money prices. To be 'effective', prices had to be established independently in the competitive 'struggle for economic existence' between free autonomous agents and enterprises. These prices were 'effective' in the calculation of efficiency because they were externally generated and imposed, as opposed to 'fictitious' prices assigned internally in a budgeting exercise. Budgetary calculation could only be done in one of two ways: by adherence to traditionally fixed prices – as in pre-capitalist societies; or by 'arbitrary dictatorial regulation' which prescribes 'the pattern of consumption and enforces obedience' (Weber, 1978, 104).

In general, 'money can never be merely a harmless "voucher" or a purely nominal unit of accounting so long as it is money' (Weber, 1978, 79). In the same way that bread tokens were used in Ptolemaic Egypt, the purchase of goods with vouchers given in payment for a quantity of 'socially useful labour [in a socialist economy] would follow the rules of barter exchange, not of money' (Weber, 1978, 80). Weber agreed with Neurath that Germany's organization of the First World War economy was effective; but it was also exceptional in its orientation to a single goal, under central control, using power not tolerated in peacetime except 'where the subjects are "slaves" of an authoritarian state' (Weber, 1978, 106). Consequently, he contended that a 'complete socialization' of the economy could only be effectively – but not necessarily efficiently – accomplished in an authoritarian state. Although Weber didn't pursue the question, this strongly implies that any socialist or communist system would lack dynamism in a way comparable to the bureaucratic empires of Ptolemaic Egypt and ancient Babylon (Weber, 1978, 1094–7). Weber has history on his side in arguing that money as an instrument for the effective creation of the objective valuation of resources requires a social structure which enables a rule-governed 'struggle for economic existence'. His analysis suggests that making money scarce enough to avoid inflation requires a competitive but relatively equal balance of power between interests. In late twentieth-century capitalism, for example, the concentration of power enabled organized labour and monopoly capital to make escalating claims which induced a 'wage–price' spiral. Since the abandonment of Bretton Woods, speculation on global capital and foreign currency markets has caused volatility and uncertainty, on the one hand, but, on the other, it has been able to 'keep governments honest' by responding to potentially inflationary spending (Pettifor, 2017). Where there is almost complete monopoly control of money in authoritarian command economies, prices cannot be established in a competitive struggle and money is unable effectively to perform its functions. Where production and consumption are centrally controlled, money can become increasingly meaningless as a means of economic calculation, means of payment, and store of value (see Woodruff, 1999, chap. 3).

If we follow Weber, the outlook for large-scale modern societies remains bleak. Alternatives to the competitive struggle are either a pervasive value consensus by which collective goals are agreed – that is, communitarian utopias and maybe earlier small traditional societies – or unworkable centralized command societies. His analysis should not be taken as an endorsement of existing capitalist society and its unequal distribution of power and wealth; but it should be considered in schemes for remedying its flawed monetary system.

8
Conclusions

The old debates persist, but there are signs that a better understanding of money is gradually becoming more widely known. One landmark was the acknowledgement of 'endogenous' money creation by the banking system in the *Bank of England Quarterly Bulletin* (McLeay et al., 2014) with its implicit acceptance of the credit theory of money. However, it must not be forgotten that this conception of money had been available in sociology and heterodox schools of economics since the nineteenth century (Ingham, 2004). And it is not surprising to find that bankers have always been aware of how money is produced as a credit–debt relation (Hodgson, 2015). It is, therefore, disappointing to find that mainstream economics textbooks have yet fully to incorporate this understanding of money. The tenet of money's long-run neutrality and the sharp distinction between 'money' and 'credit' remain part of the basic education of students of economics. Of course, as Thomas Kuhn explained in *The Structure of Scientific Revolutions*, inertia is built into academia; the establishment clings to its prestigious intellectual framework, passing it on the next generation (Kuhn, 1962). Despite the anomalies and difficulties, 'neutral' money is an integrally logical component of neoclassical microeconomics, general equilibrium theory, and the macroeconomics that replaced Keynesian economics in the late twentieth century. Credit and state theories of money could not be fully accepted without damaging repercussions for models which are ultimately based on the assumptions of 'neutral' money and the 'real' economy (for alternative macroeconomic models of capitalism based on 'credit' and 'state' theories of money, see Smithin, 2018).

The widespread realization that mainstream economic models were disabled by their omission of money and finance from comprehending the GFC and other developments in modern economies has led a resurgence of interest in Keynes (Skidelsky, 2018). His attempt to at least substantially modify the dominant classical orthodoxy of 'neutral' money and the 'real' economy was ultimately rejected. Orthodoxy lost some ground after 1945 but regained most of it following the crises of the 1970s. For Keynes, the 'classical' model was of a 'cooperative economy' based on the exchange of commodities, with or without a medium of exchange, to satisfy individual 'utility': that is, the Commodity–Money–Commodity sequence in Smith's and Marx's depiction of pre-capitalist exchange. In a similar way to Marx and Weber, Keynes understood that capitalism was a 'monetary production economy' in which the central dynamic was the employment of money-capital to make money-profit: Money–Commodity–Money$_1$ (Keynes, 1973 [1933]; Smithin, 2018).

The two kinds of economic analysis and their respective theories of money lie behind the most contested question in the governance of capitalism. On the one hand, mainstream economics believes that the supply of money *cannot* and therefore *should not* be allowed to exceed the economy's productive capacity in the long run. Only 'real' forces of production – technology, labour – create new value; and their input cannot be increased simply by injections of money. Consequently, if monetary expansion runs ahead of these 'real' forces, inflation inevitably follows. On the other hand, the broadly Keynesian and heterodox tradition continues to argue that money is the vital productive resource – a 'social technology' – that can be used to create non-inflationary economic growth and employment. However, to be effective, this must be done not by injections of 'quantities' of money but by being spent into existence. If private enterprise is incapable of the full utilization of all available resources in the 'real' economy – including labour – then it falls to government to spend on goods and services in order to make this possible.

The barriers to the reinstating of this broadly Keynesian project are entrenched in the intellectual, institutional, and ideological separation of the 'fiscal' and the 'monetary' by which the latter is removed from democratic government control. The present regime for the governance of capitalism requires, first, that government fiscal policy must attempt to balance tax revenue and expenditure, and, second, that central banks, in their independent 'state of exception', must attempt to calibrate the supply of money in relation to the productive capacity of the economy, as calculated by expert macroeconomic models. As we have seen, this has reached its apogee in the ECB's control of the euro.

In short, the money question has two elements: first, an adequate theory of money – what it is and how it is produced; and, second, the essential political dimension – who controls the production of money; how much; to what ends? In a modern democracy, how can agreement on the aims of monetary policy be achieved and implemented? For example, given irreconcilable conflicts of interest, is the location of monetary control in agencies – central banks and global money markets – outside the democratic arena the only means of establishing stable money?

What do we know after millennia of debate and dispute, and what can be done? Despite the persistent ideological attempts to assign money to the natural world – or at least outside the social realm – it has been known since money was first used that it is a 'social technology' that can stimulate economic activity as a 'force' of production. We also know that large increases in the supply of money, or, more accurately, large increases to finance government expenditure, can cause inflation. However, any transition from mild inflation to hyperinflation is invariably the result of political instability and loss of legitimacy, which destroys confidence in purchasing power. The crux of the matter is whether creating and spending money is aimed at maintaining the necessary level of effective demand to use all existing resources and encourage the production of new ones. Whether this can be achieved depends, in the first instance, on the choice of economic theory and conception of money that informs the models making the prognosis.

Wartime economies have shown that expenditure can achieve the non-inflationary full use of resources and employment; but they were based on political conditions that are not found in liberal democracies in peacetime. Planned production, directed labour, prices and incomes controls, and rationing in the Second World War were authoritarian – as Weber would have acknowledged. But, as we saw in chapter 4, the experience paved the way for a short-lived social and political agreement between the main interests, brought about by wartime shifts in the balance of power between capital and states – both domestically and globally – to pursue full employment and accept a more equitable distribution of resources. Unfortunately, the present state of world capitalism is as inimical as it could be for a second attempt.

Further Reading

Calomiris, C. and S. Haber (2014). *Fragile by Design: The Political Origins of Banking Crises and Scarce Credit.* Princeton: Princeton University Press.
The single most comprehensive account of the political history of the development of modern monetary systems.

Dodd, N. (2014). *The Social Life of Money.* Princeton: Princeton University Press.
Immensely scholarly and wide-ranging – but accessible – account of every conceivable analysis of money from a wide range of disciplines.

Ingham, G. (2004). *The Nature of Money.* Cambridge: Polity.
Detailed account of orthodox and heterodox economic monetary theory and the history and sociology of money.

Ingham, G. (ed.) (2005). *Concepts of Money: Interdisciplinary Perspectives from Economics, Sociology and Political Science.* Cheltenham: Edward Elgar.
Contains thirty-five reprinted articles and extracts from the work of the major writers referred to in the present book.

Martin, F. (2013). *Money: The Unauthorized Biography.* New York: Alfred A. Knopf.
An engaging, entertaining, erudite historical and theoretical analysis.

Orléan, A. (2014). *The Empire of Value: A New Foundation for Economics*. Cambridge, MA: MIT Press.
Contains an analysis of money as a social institution, which forms the basis for an incisive critique of orthodox mainstream economics.

Pettifor, A. (2017). *The Production of Money: How to Break the Power of Bankers*. London: Verso.
Concise, clear, and impassioned tract on the politics of money creation.

Skidelsky, R. (2018). *Money and Government: A Challenge to Mainstream Economics*. London: Allen Lane.
The culmination of a lifetime's work on the great John Maynard Keynes, which is applied to the theory of money, the history of economic and monetary policy, and a withering Keynesian critique of orthodoxy. If this proves a little difficult, try his *Keynes: The Return of the Master* (London: Allen Lane, 2009).

Smithin, J. (2018). *Rethinking the Theory of Money, Credit, and Macroeconomics: A New Statement for the Twenty-First Century*. Lanham, MD: Lexington Books.
A Keynesian-inspired, heterodox monetary analysis of capitalism which also uses econometric methods to present alternative models to mainstream economic orthodoxy analysis and policy.

Wray, L. R. (2012). *Modern Money Theory: A Primer on Macroeconomics for Sovereign Monetary Systems*. London: Palgrave Macmillan.
Lively, accessible account of Modern Monetary Theory by its most prolific exponent.

References

Ahamed, L. (2009). *Lords of Finance: 1929, the Great Depression, and the Bankers Who Broke the World*. London: Heinemann.

Aquanno, S. and J. Brennan (2016). 'Some inflationary aspects of distributional conflict', *Journal of Economic Issues*, 50, 1, 217–44.

Arrighi, G. (1994). *The Long Twentieth Century: Money, Power and the Origins of Our Time*. London: Verso.

Authers, J. (2017). 'Lessons from the Quant Quake resonate a decade later', *Financial Times*, 18 August.

Bagehot, W. (1873). *Lombard Street: A Description of the Money Market*. New York: Scribner, Armstrong & Co.

Bell, S. (2001). 'The role of the state in the hierarchy of money'. *Cambridge Journal of Economics*. 25, 149-163.

Bell, S. A. and E. J. Nell (eds) (2003). *The State, the Market and the Euro*. Cheltenham: Edward Elgar.

Benes, J. and M. Kumhof (2012) 'The Chicago Plan revisited'. IMF working paper (WP/12/202). Online at: *https://www.imf.org/external/pubs/ft/wp/2012/wp12202.pdf*

Bloch, M. (1954 [1936]). *Esquisse d'une histoire monétaire de l'Europe*. Paris: Armand Colin.

Boettke, P. (2000). *Socialism and the Market: The Socialist Calculation Debate Revisited*. London: Routledge Library of 20th Century Economics.

Boyer-Xambeu, M., G. Delaplace and L. Gillard (1994). *Private Money and Public Currencies: The Sixteenth Century Challenge*. London: M. E. Sharpe.

Brewer, J. (1989). *The Sinews of Power: War, Money and the English State, 1688–1783.* London: Unwin.

Buchan, J. (1997). *Frozen Desire: An Enquiry into the Meaning of Money.* London: Picador.

Buiter, W. (2009). 'The unfortunate uselessness of most "state of the art" academic monetary economics'. VOXeu.org, 6 March. Online at: *https://mpra.ub.uni-muenchen.de/58407/1/MPRA_paper_58407.pdf*

Burn, G. (2006). *The Re-emergence of Global Finance.* Basingstoke: Palgrave Macmillan.

Calomiris, C. and S. Haber (2014). *Fragile by Design: The Political Origins of Banking Crises and Scarce Credit.* Princeton: Princeton University Press.

Carruthers, B. and S. Babb (1996). 'The colour of money and the nature of value: greenbacks and gold in post-bellum America'. Reprinted in G. Ingham (ed.), *Concepts of Money: Interdisciplinary Perspectives from Economics, Sociology and Political Science.* Cheltenham: Edward Elgar, 2005.

Cartelier, J. (2007). 'The hypostasis of money: an economic point of view', *Cambridge Journal of Economics*, 31, 2, 217–33.

Crouch, C. (2009). 'Privatised Keynesianism: an unacknowledged policy regime', *The British Journal of Politics and International Relations*, 11, 382–99.

Davies, G. (1996). *A History of Money.* Cardiff: University of Wales Press.

de Cecco, M. (1974). *Money and Empire: The International Gold Standard, 1890–1914.* Oxford: Blackwell.

Del Mar, A. (1901). *A History of Monetary Systems.* New York: The Cambridge Encyclopaedia Company. (Originally published as *The Science of Money.* London: Bell and Sons, 1895.)

Desan, C. (2014). *Making Money: Coin, Currency, and the Coming of Capitalism.* Oxford: Oxford University Press.

Devine, P. (2010). *Democracy and Planning*, Cambridge: Polity.

Dodd, N. (2014). *The Social Life of Money.* Princeton: Princeton University Press.

Dyson, B. G. Hodgson, and F. van Lerven (2016). *Sovereign Money: An Introduction.* London: Positive Money. Online at: *http://positivemoney.org/wp-content/uploads/2016/12/Sovereign Money-AnIntroduction-20161214.pdf*

Eichengreen, B. (1995). *Golden Fetters: The Gold Standard and the Great Depression.* Oxford: Oxford University Press.

Eichengreen, B. (2010). *Exorbitant Privilege: The Rise and Fall of the Dollar and the Future of the International Monetary System.* Oxford: Oxford University Press.

Einaudi, L. (1936]. 'The theory of imaginary money from Charlemagne to the French Revolution'. Reprinted in G. Ingham (ed.), *Concepts of Money: Interdisciplinary Perspectives from Economics, Sociology and Political Science*. Cheltenham: Edward Elgar, 2005.

Ellman, M. (2014). *Socialist Planning*, third edition. Cambridge: Cambridge University Press.

Evans, R. J. (2002). *The Coming of the Third Reich, 1919–1945*. London: Penguin.

Fantacci, L. (2008). 'The dual currency system of Renaissance Europe'. *Financial History Review*, 15, 1, 55–72.

Feldman, G. (1996). *The Great Disorder: Politics, Economics and Society in the German Inflation, 1919–1924*. Oxford: Oxford University Press.

Fergusson, A. (2010 [1975]). *When Money Dies: The Nightmare of the Weimar Hyper-Inflation*. London: Old Street Publishing.

Fisher, I. (1911). *The Purchasing Power of Money: Its Determination and Relation to Credit Interest and Crises*. New York: Macmillan.

Fox, D. (2011). 'The case of mixt monies'. *The Cambridge Law Journal*, 70, 1, 144–74.

Fox, D. and W. Ernst (eds) (2016). *Money in the Western Legal Tradition: Middle Ages to Bretton Woods*. Oxford: Oxford University Press.

Friedman, M. (1970). *The Counter-Revolution in Monetary Theory*. London: The Wincott Institute for Economic Affairs.

Gatch, L. (2012). 'Tax anticipation scrip as a form of local currency in the USA during the 1930s'. *International Journal of Community Currency Research*, 16, Section D, 22–35.

Goodhart, C. (2003 [1998]). 'The two concepts of money: implications for optimum currency areas'. In S. A. Bell and E. J. Nell (eds), *The State, the Market and the Euro*. Cheltenham: Edward Elgar.

Goodhart, C. (2009). 'The continuing muddles of monetary theory: a steadfast refusal to face facts'. *Economica*, 76, 820–30.

Gowan, P. (1999). *The Global Gamble: Washington's Faustian Bid for World Dominance*. London: Verso.

Graeber, D. (2011). *Debt: The First 5,000 Years*. New York: Melville House.

Grierson, P. (1977). *The Origins of Money*. London: Athlone Press.

Hager, S. (2016). *Public Debt, Inequality, and Power: The Making of a Modern Debt State*. Oakland: University of California Press.

Hahn, F. (1987). 'Foundations of monetary theory'. In M. de Cecco and J. P. Fitoussi (eds), *Monetary Theory and Economic Institutions*. London: Macmillan.

Hart, K. (2000). *The Memory Bank: Money in an Unequal World*. London: Profile Books.

Hayek F. (1976). *Denationalization of Money: An Analysis of the Theory and Practice of Competitive Currencies*. London: Institute of Economic Affairs.

Hayek, F. (1994 [1944]). *The Road to Serfdom*. Chicago: University of Chicago Press.

Helleiner, E. (1994). *States and the Reemergence of Global Finance: From Bretton Woods to the 1990s*. Ithaca, NY: Cornell University Press.

Hicks, J. R. (1989). *A Market Theory of Money*. Oxford: Oxford University Press

Hodgson, G. M. (2015). *Conceptualizing Capitalism: Institutions, Evolution, Future*. Chicago: University of Chicago Press

Hopkins, K. (1978). *Conquerors and Slaves*. Cambridge: Cambridge University Press.

Huber, J. (2017). *Sovereign Money: Beyond Reserve Banking*. London: Palgrave.

Hull, C. H. (ed.) (1997 [1899]). *The Economic Writings of Sir William Petty*. London: Routledge.

Hung, H.-f. and R. Thompson (2016). 'Money supply, class power, and inflation: monetarism reassessed'. *American Sociological Review*, 81, 3, 447–66.

Ingham, G. (1984). *Capitalism Divided? The City and Industry in British Social Development*. London: Macmillan.

Ingham, G. (2004). *The Nature of Money*. Cambridge: Polity.

Ingham, G. (2005). 'Introduction'. In G. Ingham (ed.), *Concepts of Money: Interdisciplinary Perspectives from Economics, Sociology and Political Science*. Cheltenham: Edward Elgar.

Ingham, G. (2006). 'Further reflections on the ontology of money: responses to Lapavitsas and Dodd'. *Economy and Society*, 35, 2, 259–78.

Ingham, G. (2011). *Capitalism*. Cambridge: Polity.

Ingham, G. (2015). '"The Great Divergence": Max Weber and China's "missing links"'. *Max Weber Studies*, 15, 2, 1–32.

Ingham, G. (2019). 'Max Weber: money, credit and finance in capitalism'. In E. Hanke, L. Scaff, and S. Whimster (eds), *The Oxford Handbook of Max Weber*. Oxford: Oxford University Press.

Ingham, G., K. Coutts, and S. Konzelmann (eds) (2016). '"Cranks" and "Brave Heretics": Re-thinking Money and Banking after the Great Financial Crisis'. *Cambridge Journal of Economics, Special Issue*, 40, 5.

Jackson, K. (1995). *The Oxford Book of Money*. Oxford: Oxford University Press.

Kalecki, M. (1943). 'Political aspects of full employment'. *Political Quarterly*, 14, 322–31.

Keynes, J. M. (1930). *A Treatise on Money*. London: Macmillan.

Keynes, J. M. (1931). 'The pure theory of money: a reply to Dr Hayek'. *Economica*, 34, 387–97.

Keynes, J. M. (1971 [1923]) *A Tract on Monetary Reform. Collected Writings of John Maynard Keynes*, Vol. IV (ed. D. Moggridge). Cambridge: Cambridge University Press.

Keynes, J. M. (1973 [1933]). 'A monetary theory of production'. In *Collected Writings of John Maynard Keynes*, Vol. XXI (ed. D. Moggridge). Cambridge: Cambridge University Press.

Keynes, J. M. (1973 [1936]). *The General Theory of Employment, Interest and Money*. Cambridge: Cambridge University Press.

Keynes, J. M. (1978). 'From Cabinet agreement to White Paper, 1942–3'. In *Collected Writings of John Maynard Keynes*, Vol. XXV. (eds E. Johnson and D. Moggeridge). Cambridge: Cambridge University Press.

King, M. (2017). *The End of Alchemy: Money, Banking and the Future of the Global Economy*. London: Abacus.

Knapp, G. (1973 [1905]). *The State Theory of Money*. New York: Augustus Kelly.

Kuhn T. S. (1962). *The Structure of Scientific Revolutions*. Chicago: University of Chicago Press.

Lapavitsas, C. (2005). 'The social relation of money as the universal equivalent: a response to Ingham'. *Economy and Society*, 34, 3, 389–403.

Lapavitsas, C. (2016). *Marxist Monetary Theory: Collected Papers*. Leiden: Brill.

Lerner, A. (1943). 'Functional finance and the federal debt'. *Social Research*, 10, 38–51.

Levy, D. M. and S. J. Peart (2008). 'Socialist calculation debate'. In *The New Palgrave Dictionary of Economics*, second edition (eds S. N. Durlauf and L. E. Blume). Basingstoke: Palgrave Macmillan. Online at: *https://link.springer.com/content/pdf/10. 1057%2F978-1-349-95121-5_2070-1.pdf*

Lietaer, B. and J. Dunne (2013). *Rethinking Money*. Oakland, CA: Berrett-Koehler Publishers.

Lipsey, R. and A. Chrystal (2011). *Economics*, twelfth edition. Oxford: Oxford University Press

Lucarelli, S. and L. Gobbi (2016). 'Local clearing unions as stabilizers of local economic systems: a stock flow consistent perspective'. In G. Ingham, K. Coutts, and S. Konzelmann (eds), '"Cranks" and "brave heretics": re-thinking money and banking after the

Great Financial Crisis'. *Cambridge Journal of Economics, Special Issue*, 40, 5, 1397–420.

Macfarlane, L., J. Ryan-Collins, O. Bjerg, R. Nielsen, and D. McCann (2017). 'Making money from making money: seigniorage in the modern economy'. Copenhagen Business School Working Paper. Online at: *https://openarchive.cbs.dk/bitstream/handle/10398/9470/nef_making_money_from_making_money.pdf?sequence=1*

Mankiw, N. and M. Taylor (2008). *Macroeconomics*, second edition. Basingstoke: Palgrave Macmillan.

Mankiw, N. and M. Taylor (2017). *Macroeconomics*, fourth edition. Andover: Cengage Learning.

Mann, G. (2013). 'The monetary exception: labour, distribution and money in capitalism'. *Capital and Class*, 37, 2, 197–216.

Martin, F. (2013). *Money: The Unauthorized Biography*. New York: Alfred A. Knopf.

Marx, K. (1976 [1867]). *Capital*, Vol. 1 (trans. B. Fowkes). Harmondsworth: Penguin.

Marx, K. (1981 [1887]). *Capital*, Vol. 3 (trans. D. Fernbach). Harmondsworth: Penguin.

McLeay, M., A. Radia, and R. Thomas (2014). 'Money in the modern economy: an introduction', *Bank of England Quarterly Bulletin* Q1. Online at: *https://www.bankofengland.co.uk/quarterly-bulletin/2014/q1/money-in-the-modern-economy-an-introduction*

Mehrling, P. (2011). *The New Lombard Street: How the Fed Became the Dealer of Last Resort*. Princeton: Princeton University Press.

Menger, C. (1892). 'On the origins of money'. *Economic Journal*, 2, 6, 239–55.

Minsky, H. P. (1982). 'The financial instability hypothesis'. In C. Kindleberger and J.-P. Laffargue (eds), *Financial Crises: Theory, History & Policy*. Cambridge: Cambridge University Press.

Minsky, H. P. (2008 [1986]). *Stabilizing an Unstable Economy*. New York: McGraw Hill.

Mirowski, P. (1991). 'Post-modernism and the social theory of value'. *Journal of Post Keynesian Economics*, 13, 562–82.

Mitchell Innes, A. (1914). 'The credit theory of money'. Reprinted in G. Ingham (ed.), *Concepts of Money: Interdisciplinary Perspectives from Economics, Sociology and Political Science*. Cheltenham: Edward Elgar, 2005.

Moe, T. (2018). 'Financial stability and money creation: a review of Morgan Ricks: *The Money Problem*'. *Accounting, Economics, and Law: A Convivium* 8, 2, 1–13.

Nersisyan, Y. and L. R. Wray (2016) 'Modern Money Theory and the facts of experience'. In G. Ingham, K. Coutts, and

S. Konzelmann (eds), '"Cranks" and "brave heretics": re-thinking money and banking after the Great Financial Crisis'. *Cambridge Journal of Economics, Special Issue*, 40, 5, 1297–316.

North, P. (2007). *Money and Liberation: The Micropolitics of Alternative Currency Movements*. Minneapolis: University of Minnesota Press.

Orléan, A. (2008), 'La crise monétaire en allemande des années 1920'. In B. Théret, *La monnaie dévoilée par ses crises. Vol. II: Crises monétaires en Russie et en Allemagne au XXe siècle*. Paris: Éditions de l'EHESS.

Orléan, A. (2014a). 'Money: instrument of exchange or social institution of value?' In J. Pixley and G. Harcourt (eds), *Financial Crises and the Nature of Capitalist Money: Mutual Developments from the Work of Geoffrey Ingham*. Basingstoke: Palgrave Macmillan.

Orléan, A. (2014b). *The Empire of Value: A New Foundation for Economics* (trans. M. B. DeBevoise). Cambridge, MA: MIT Press.

Otero-Iglesias, M. (2015). 'Stateless euro: the euro crisis and the revenge of the chartalist theory of money'. *Journal of Common Market Studies*, 53, 2, 349–64.

Peacock, M. (2013). *Introducing Money*. London: Routledge.

Pettifor, A. (2017). *The Production of Money: How to Break the Power of Bankers*. London: Verso.

Phillips, L. and M. Rozworksi (2019). *People's Republic of Walmart: How the World's Biggest Corporations are Laying the Foundation for Socialism*. London: Verso.

Pixley, J. (2018). *Central Banks, Democratic States and Financial Power*. Cambridge: Cambridge University Press.

Polanyi, K., C. M. Arensberg, and H. W. Pearson (eds) (1957). *Trade and Market in the Early Empires*. New York: Free Press.

Radford, R. A. (1945). 'The economic organisation of a POW camp'. Reprinted in G. Ingham (ed.), *Concepts of Money: Interdisciplinary Perspectives from Economics, Sociology and Political Science*. Cheltenham: Edward Elgar, 2005.

Reinhart, C. and M. Belen Sbrancia (2011). 'The liquidation of government debt'. NBER Working Paper 16893. Cambridge, MA: National Bureau of Economic Research. Online at: *https://www.imf.org/external/pubs/ft/wp/2015/wp1507.pdf*

Ricks, M. (2016). *The Money Problem: Rethinking Financial Regulation*. Chicago: University of Chicago Press.

Robertson, D. (1948 [1928]). *Money*. London: Nisbet.

Rowthorn, R. (1977). 'Conflict, inflation and money'. *Cambridge Journal of Economics*, 1, 3, 215–39.

Ryan-Collins, J., T. Greenham, R. Werner, and A. Jackson (2011).

Where Does Money Come From? A Guide to the UK Monetary and Banking System. London: New Economics Foundation.

Saiag, H. (2019). 'Money as a social relation beyond the state: a contribution to the institutionalist approach based on the Argentinian *trueque*'. *The British Journal of Sociology*, 70, 3, 969–96.

Sargent, T. and N. Wallace (1975) 'Rational expectations, the optimum policy instrument and optimum money supply rule'. *Journal of Political Economy*, 83, 2, 241–54.

Schmitt, C. (2005). *Political Theology: Four Chapters on the Concept of Sovereignty* (trans. G. Schwab). Chicago and London: University of Chicago Press.

Schumpeter, J. (1917). 'Money and the social product'. *International Economic Papers*, Vol. 6. London: Macmillan.

Schumpeter, J. (1934). *The Theory of Economic Development*. Cambridge, MA: Harvard University Press.

Schumpeter, J. (1994 [1954]). *History of Economic Analysis*. London: Routledge.

Searle, J. (1995). *The Construction of Social Reality*. New York: Free Press.

Simmel, G. (1978 [1907]). *The Philosophy of Money* (trans. D. Frisby). London: Routledge.

Skidelsky, R. (2018). *Money and Government: A Challenge to Mainstream Economics*. London: Allen Lane.

Smithin, J. (1996). *Macroeconomic Policy and the Future of Capitalism: The Revenge of the Rentier and the Threat to Prosperity*. Aldershot: Edward Elgar.

Smithin, J. (2018). *Rethinking the Theory of Money, Credit, and Macroeconomics: A New Statement for the Twenty-First Century*. Lanham, MD: Lexington Books.

Streeck, W. (2014). *Buying Time: The Delayed Crisis of Democratic Capitalism*. London: Verso.

Théret, B. (2017). 'Monetary federalism as a concept and its empirical underpinnings in Argentina's monetary history'. In G. Gomez (ed.), *Monetary Plurality in Local, Regional and Global Economies*. Abingdon: Routledge.

Tucker, P. (2018). *Unelected Power: The Quest for Legitimacy in Central Banking and the Regulatory State*. Princeton: Princeton University Press.

Turner, A. (2016). *Between Debt and the Devil: Money, Credit and Fixing Global Finance*. Princeton: Princeton University Press.

Tymoigne, E. (2016). 'Government monetary and fiscal operations: generalising the endogenous money approach'. *Cambridge Journal of Economics*, 40, 1317–32.

Varoufakis, G. (2017). *Adults in the Room: My Battle with Europe's Deep Establishment*. London: Random House.

Vogl, J. (2017). *The Ascendancy of Finance*. Cambridge: Polity.

Volscho, T. (2017). 'The revenge of the capitalist class: crisis, the legitimacy of capitalism and the restoration of finance from the 1970s to present'. *Critical Sociology*, 43, 2, 249–66.

von Glahn, R. (1996). *Fountain of Fortune: Money and Monetary Policy in China, 1000–1700*. Berkeley: University of California Press.

von Mises, L. (1990 [1920]). *Economic Calculation in the Socialist Commonwealth* (trans. S. Adler). Auburn, AL: Ludwig von Mises Institute.

Weber, M. (1978). *Economy and Society* (ed. G. Roth and C. Wittich). Berkeley: University of California Press.

Wennerlind, C. (2011). *The Casualties of Credit: The English Financial Revolution, 1620–1720*. Cambridge, MA: Harvard University Press.

Wolf, M. (2014). *The Shifts and the Shocks: What we have learned and have still to learn from the Financial Crisis*. London: Allen Lane.

Woodruff, D. (1999). *Money Unmade: Barter and the Fate of Russian Capitalism*. Ithaca, NY: Cornell University Press.

Woodruff, D. (2013). 'Monetary surrogates and money's dual nature'. In J. Pixley and G. Harcourt (eds), *Financial Crises and the Nature of Capitalist Money: Mutual Developments from the Work of Geoffrey Ingham*. Basingstoke: Palgrave Macmillan.

Wray, L. R. (2012). *Modern Money Theory: A Primer on Macroeconomics for Sovereign Monetary Systems*. London: Palgrave Macmillan.

Zarlenga, S. A. (2002). *Lost Science of Money: The Mythology of Money – The Story of Power*. Valatie, NY: American Monetary Institute.

Index